Ackno

To my wife, Crystal, for being a trusted friend, devoted encourager, and passionate educator. You choose the tougher road, confident and committed, always striving to achieve your goals.

To my kids for their patience in the tight times, hunger to learn, and trust in me as their provider.

To my team members, for including me in our quest to take the very best care of our customers.

To Ken, Fabian, Nicole, and Mark. Your inspiration and advice were instrumental in my quest to add value to others.

To Tiffany, John, Joe, Bill, Ken, Kary, Pat, Chris, Sharon, Chaz, and Jon—our conversations were inspiring, insightful, and impacting. Thank you!

To all those who have cheered me on to complete this book.

Most of all, to my heavenly Father, for His abundant kindness; every day is an opportunity to do my best for His glory.

2

Recommendations

"This is a wonderful, life-changing book that shows you how to decide exactly what you want and achieve more than ever before!"

---Brian Tracy – Best-Selling Author, International Speaker, Business Consultant

"In order to Win customers for life your team members need to be Winning at Life. John's book, *Winning Secrets*, reveals how we can all Win more at Life."

---Shep Hyken, New York Times bestselling author of *The Amazement Revolution*

"The strategies in *Winning Secrets* will help you develop a growth mindset that leads to more Wins, each and every day."

---David Meltzer, Co-Founder Sports 1 Marketing, Consultant, Business Coach, Keynote Speaker, 3x Best Selling Author

"I am very passionate about helping people become their true selves so they can make a bigger impact on the world. John has written a beautiful book to help you get a few steps closer to that goal, if not all the way there."

---Gino Wickman, Author of *Traction*, creator of *EOS* and *The Ten Disciplines for Managing and Maximizing Your Energy*

"In this book, John D. Hanson, shows you step by step how you can live an extraordinary life so countless others will as a result."

---John R. DiJulius III, Author of *The Customer Service Revolution*

"In a world full of constant challenges, unrealistic expectations, and criticism, John's book, *Winning Secrets*, is a breath of fresh air. Encouraging, inspiring, motivating, and insightful, his proven principles and fresh ideas will empower you to continue chasing your dreams. As a speaker and author, I realized that the challenging years in the past equipped me to deliver life-changing impact now. Read this book to discover how you too can Win at Life now, to help others Win in the future."

---Marcus Sheridan, Business Owner, Entrepreneur, International Speaker, Author of *They Ask, You Answer*

"John D. Hanson's *Winning Secrets* is your opportunity to begin your Success journey in new and unexpected ways. Read it, and begin to Win like never before."

---Skip Prichard, Author of *The Book of Mistakes: 9 Secrets to Creating a Successful Future*; CEO, OCLC, Inc.

"*Winning Secrets* is a remarkably inspiring and empowering resource for achieving life and business Success. In it, John D. Hanson offers keen insights on what it means to 'Win', principles for interpersonal impact, and pragmatic & actionable tools. Buy this book, and change your destiny!"

---Joseph Michelli, Ph.D. New York Times #1 bestselling author of books like *The Airbnb Way* and *Leading the Starbucks Way*

"John is a leader dedicated to adding value to others. His book is a reflection of his heart to help people succeed. Get ready to Win in a bigger way."

---Dr. Kary Oberbrunner, WSJ and USA Today bestselling author

"Winning isn't an end. It's a pursuit...a mindset...a lifestyle. And EVERYONE has the ability to achieve it. It isn't limited to your background, family, education, or anything else you thought would accelerate or stall your progress.

Winners Win. And you're a Winner. You may just not be living like it...yet.

Meet John. John writes in a delightful style with inspiring stories, encouraging thoughts and extremely practical advice you can (and should) practice today. It's a Masterclass on Winning, complete with moments for reflection, action steps, and tips from other Winners. Read to Win!"

---Bill Montgomery, CEO of River Radio Ministries, Adjunct Professor of Management/Sales

"John's book is worth a read. His ten Winning secrets are not new - they've just been mostly forgotten. John's approachable style and timeless truths will change you if you let them in."

---Chet Scott, Owner of Built to Lead, Coach, Author, builttolead.com

"We each only get one chance at life. John shows how to live yours to the fullest."
---David Meerman Scott, international bestselling author of 12 books including *The New Rules of Marketing and PR*

"Winning Secrets" is an Inside-Out book. The better we take care of ourselves and strengthen our inner mastery, the more effective and productive we are in the work world. Love it!"

---Alex Freytag, co-author *Profit Works*, Visionary, Expert EOS Implementer

"To begin, you must look within - and John is the perfect example of a leader who preaches what he practices, and practices what he preaches. His words inspire you to take action, and I firmly believe that this book will undoubtedly help you to grow both personally and professionally."

---Craig M. Chavis Jr, Award-Winning author & Founder, Solo Creator Club

"This book is a Winner. No pun intended. It offers a roadmap to Winning ... but not just for the select, ultra gifted/lucky/hardworking few ... but for EVERYONE. You'll take away insights (as I have) that will provide you with a new perspective and renewed motivation to continue your on Winning ways. Yes, continue. Like this book shares (and is): You're already a Winner."

---Frank Agin, Founder & President of AmSpirit Business Connections, www.frankagin.com

"Heroic Success.....John's book helped me with truly understanding what WINNING is all about!"

---Gary Russell, Founder/CEO of Winning Profile, Inc., Talent Strategist

"What do you get if you were to mix Dan Sullivan with Mr. Rogers and added a sprinkling of Steve Martin?

You get a fabulous contribution by John D. Hanson, *Winning Secrets.* Centered on common sense, down-to-earth self-reflection, self-evaluation, and self-discovery, *Winning Secrets* will challenge you to think differently about what it takes to Succeed in life (and work).

Hanson's poignant and easy-to-read case stories, punctuated with humor, highlight practical approaches to his Winning secrets. His points, while pulling and tugging at your heartstrings, are punctuated by **Do It Now** Call To Actions, making this book not only thought provoking but actionable.

If you ever felt that other people were better humans than you.... give your head a shake and read this book... and Win more at Life."

---Marc Haine, Speaker, Consultant, Author of *LIGHTS! CAMERA! ACTION! Business Operational Excellence Through the Lens of Live Theatre*

"What resonates with me is truth. As I read *Winning Secrets,* I knew John was sharing truth! That's because much of what he writes about, I've experienced throughout my career of nearly 40 years and in 35 years of marriage. Put into practice the tips John shares, and you will Win in business and life."

---Brian Ahearn, CMCT, Founder of Influence PEOPLE, LLC and author of *Influence PEOPLE, Persuasive Selling,* and *The Influencer*

"This book reframes Winning and how we've been thinking about in a way that is both inspirational and accessible. John's way of framing Success should be considered by all those leaders and aspiring leaders out there who want more from their career and their life outside work."

---Greg Kihlström - Bestselling Author, Consultant, Business Advisor

"Winning Secrets is a book that focuses on personal growth and self-improvement. John D. Hanson emphasizes the importance of changing the way we see ourselves and the world around us. By changing our mindset, we can change our destiny. The book is filled with practical advice and real-life examples, making it a valuable resource for anyone looking to improve their life. *Winning Secrets* is an inspiring read that encourages readers to take control of their lives and make positive changes."

---Nick Glimsdahl, Speaker, Author, Podcast Host--*Press 1 for Nick*

"In his new book, *Winning Secrets*, John D. Hanson makes the powerful point that Winning doesn't have to involve someone else losing. This singular thought could change businesses, politics, athletes, and countless individual lives. Start your Winning journey by picking up his book today!"

---Dan Gingiss, Customer Experience keynote speaker, author of *The Experience Maker*

"Many years ago, I learned to be very careful about who got to 'speak' into my life. Oh, I'll talk to anybody, but to 'speak' to me, I have to trust you and your ideas. John D. Hanson's book, *Winning Secrets*, is a great read from a trusted friend I enjoy having 'speak' to me anytime. You'll enjoy it, too."

---Terry Dismore, Consultant, Podcast Host of Quiz the Diz

"A critical aspect of effective networking is the ability to genuinely earn trust. John's book helps us identify the ideal people to work with, as we pursue our dreams. My mission is to help people around the world, achieve their personal and professional goals by working well with others. This book will help you and all those around you Win more in life, impacting countless lives. A Win/Win resource; highly recommend!"

---Chris Borja, Keynote Speaker, Virtual Event Producer, Author of "Networking Essentials for Success"; chrisborja.com

"Winning starts with yourself, meaning that Success ultimately depends on you. In *Winning Secrets*, John has masterfully paved the golden road map to Winning and prosperity. It's up to you to set the goals, develop the strategies, and put in the effort required to achieve your desired outcome.

John becomes your sherpa, your personal guide to unlocking what has always been inside you---a Winning mindset."

---Larry Levine, Best-selling Author of *Selling from the Heart*, Co-host of the Selling from the Heart Podcast

Challenging, encouraging, and practical! John presents a radical definition of Winning that will help you define Success in your own terms. He then gives an unconventional roadmap to help you accelerate your journey."
---Darrell Amy, Author of *Revenue Growth Engine*, www.DarrellAmy.com

"Winning is everything. That's a bold statement – but in business and in life, we all want to Win. John's book came across my desk at a time when I needed inspiration to do life differently. Mission accomplished. He provides a ton of great examples and moving stories that will inspire you to do life differently, too!"

---Annette Franz, CX Expert, Consultant, Speaker, and Author of *Built to Win*

"In Winning Secrets, John D. Hanson unlocks the secret to Winning in life: (re)defining what it means to Win. Whether you lead a team or want to achieve more personally, Winning Secrets will give you the perspective, the roadmap, and the motivation to WIN in every area of life."

---Adam Toporek, Customer Experience Keynote Speaker, Author of *Be Your Customer's Hero*

"We are currently living in an era of immense complexity and complications. However, it is also a period of enormous potential and opportunities. The key to accessing these opportunities lies in the application of wisdom.

In his book "Winning Secrets," John D. Hanson brilliantly explains how wisdom can be applied to achieve Success. His writing style is both simple and sincere, making the book a truly meaningful experience.

This book has the power to transform your life. It is a must-read for anyone looking to achieve Success."

---Rajiv Chelladurai, Author of Leadership Parables, Fearless in Battle, Wisdom Workout & GIFT. Leadership Coach & Facilitator

"Having a Winning mindset is essential for Success. Yet Winning isn't just about being the first, the best or the only. In this book, John shows readers how to redefine their view of Winning and how to Win more often in their everyday life."

---Nicole Jansen, Leadership Coach, Business Advisor and Podcast Host

"We are all 'Winners,' especially U.S. military members who chose to protect and defend freedom. When these Winners transition away from military service, it's tough. John's 10 Winning Secrets are highly relevant for Veterans facing these challenging times, as well as the civilian Veteran Champions who support them. Use John's principles to broaden the Veteran Champion Movement and 'be a part of the Win.'"

---Kathy Lowrey Gallowitz, Lt.Col., USAF, Retired; Author of *Beyond 'Thank You for Your Service,' The Veteran Champion Handbook for Civilians*

"Winning Secrets offers a new perspective on Success, and this has made me approach my business and life differently. A must read."

---Jonathan Daniels, Author of *The Customer Experience Playbook*;
www.cx-centric.com

"John's book is a clear and compelling call-to-action that challenges you to challenge yourself and, as the US Army likes to say, 'Be all that you can be!'"

---Jeff Sheehan, CX Advisor & Customer Service Consultant, Author of *Customer Experience Management Field Manual*

"This book will stimulate your thinking to develop your definition of what Winning and Success is to you. Loaded with wonderful stories and examples to help you become the Winner you deserve to be. If you need clarity with what Winning looks like, you need to read this book!"

---Coach Jim Johnson, Inspirational Leadership, Speaker, and Author

"John's book Winning Secrets is a great read. It is a good reminder of the importance of how to Win More at Life. John provides some great stories and examples that keep us wanting more. Thanks, John For The WIN!"

---Debbie Hart, Customer Experience Assessments Specialist, Owner of The Hart Experience; https://www.thehartexperience.com

"An emotionally gripping book that resonates with readers on a business and personal level. It evokes a wide range of thoughts about what really means "to Win" for us and for our environment. A must-read masterpiece that leaves everyone feeling inspired."

---Gregorio Uglioni, CX Goalkeeper, Podcast Host-- Switzerland

"Just reading the first 13 pages completely caught my attention! This book is very inspiring, easy to read and makes you rethink many paradigms we have built within ourselves. I can completely relate to this concept of what "Winning" really means as I've been writing about it in my LinkedIn feed to try and use my experience at Loyalty Metrics to help others "Win"."

---Rodrigo Edwards, Founder of Loyalty Metrics CX, Solopreneur Coach-Latin America

"This book throws some great new perspectives on what Winning actually means. The stories that accompany the insight and questions to trigger reflection are well selected. Thanks John, for shining a light on these ways of thinking and making sure they don't stay a secret for much longer."

--- Fred Copestake, Bestselling Author of *Hybrid Selling* and *Selling Through Partnering Skills*

"*Winning Secrets* is a powerful and understandable book. John D. Hanson has given us a clear pathway to a magnificent life of significance. Do the world a favor---buy John's book, read it, then tell others of the treasure you found."

---Pat Gano, author *Language of Heaven: 5 Gifts That Create Legacy*

"Winning secrets come from the experience of those that have embraced the process to Success. John is a leader by example that shares his experience in this book how you can embrace your process to Win big in life."

---Christopher Salem, Business Acceleration Strategist, Professional Keynote Speaker Award, Winning Author https://sustainablesuccess.net/; https://christophersalem.com/

"There are 2 kinds of moments in life: those you miss and those you seize. John Hanson's *Winning Secrets* shines a light on the many, many moments where we have opportunities to Win, but might not realize it. *Winning Secrets* emphasizes over and over that now is the time to make a shift in the paradigm of our lives and start Winning at everything we do, and John shows us how to do it."

---Jim Bass, Customer Experience Strategy and Innovation Leader

"In his insight-FULL book, John steers you in the right direction, not meandering in life, but rather setting the pace. In the end, it's a Win-Win. What do I mean by a Win-Win? Well, you'll just have to read it for yourself."

---Bill Quiseng, Chief Experience Officer, Customer Care Expert, Keynote Speaker

"Winning is relative and while we all strive to Win, there's an approach to Winning that is healthy and sustainable.

I've never really given the concept of Winning much thought until I read John's book, *Winning Secrets*. I particularly was drawn to its intimate message and could relate to its content.

John says "...an easy life doesn't mean we're doing everything right, and a challenging life doesn't mean we're doing everything wrong..." and his book explains why.

If you're like me and have a strong character and deeply held core values, you'll find truths in this book *Winning Secrets* that will change how you think about Winning. It's a must read if you really want to Win in all areas of your life."

---Debbie Akwara, CX Consultant, Pan-African Business Transformation Leader

"John D. Hanson's book, *Winning Secrets*, offers a valuable chance for individuals to reassess their personal priorities. Blending aspects of both altruism and self-interest, the book highlights the significance of focusing on one's own well-being as a means to effectively support others, ultimately leading to positive outcomes for all parties involved.

I wholeheartedly recommend John's book to individuals who are contemplating ways to elevate their lives and reach new levels of personal growth and fulfillment."

---Michael Brandt, CX Consultant, Trainer, Coach, Speaker

"John's book, *Winning Secrets*, is part personal growth and part motivation for living a fulfilling life that's told through truisms, personal stories, and practical advice. A good read for creating positive change."

---Alex Allwood, Author, *Customer Empathy* and *Customer Experience is the Brand*

Foreword

Winning is a concept that has been a part of human existence from the early days of civilization to the modern era. Winning has always been at the forefront of every human endeavor. Whether it's a battle, a game of chance, a competition, or a business venture, everyone wants to be a Winner.

But what separates the Winners from the losers?

What are the secrets to Winning?

These are the questions that have intrigued scholars, thinkers, and curious people for centuries, and these are the secrets that are revealed in, *Winning Secrets: How a Dictionary and a Ruler Can Change Your Life.*

In this book, John D. Hanson explores the secrets to Winning in all areas of life. He delves into the minds of Successful people from all walks of life and examines the common traits that make them Winners.

To write this book, John collaborated with experts in various fields and interviewed some highly-Successful people. He read countless books and articles, analyzed research studies, and distilled the essence of what it takes to Win. What emerged was a comprehensive guide to Winning that anyone can use to achieve their dreams.

You'll learn proven principles from world-class athletes like Michael Jordan and Serena Williams, who have dominated their respective sports for decades. You'll discover the secrets of respected entrepreneurs like Jeff Bezos and Elon Musk, who have built some of the most Successful businesses in the world.

But this book is not just about the famous and Successful. It's also about "ordinary people" who have achieved extraordinary things. People like Sara Blakely, who started her billion-dollar business with just $5,000 in savings and a dream.

One of the key themes throughout *Winning Secrets* is the importance of mindset.

This book emphasizes the need for a growth mindset, which involves a willingness to learn, adapt, and improve. As John eloquently illustrates, when we embrace a growth mindset, we open ourselves up to new opportunities and possibilities, and we become more resilient in the face of setbacks and challenges.

Another important factor John explores in Winning is having a clear sense of purpose. Knowing what we want to achieve and why we want to achieve it provides us with direction and motivation.

But Winning is not just about mindset and purpose - it also requires action.

John provides valuable insights into the importance of taking consistent and strategic action towards our goals. From developing good habits to taking calculated risks, *Winning Secrets* offers practical advice on how to turn our goals into reality.

One of the things that sets *Winning Secrets* apart is its focus on the importance of collaboration and community. While individual effort is certainly important, John also recognizes that we can achieve much more when we work together. He discusses the power of building strong relationships, seeking out mentors & advisors, leveraging our networks to achieve our goals and Win at life.

Throughout *Winning Secrets*, John shares his own personal stories of triumph, as well as his setbacks. This helps to humanize the concept of Winning and reminds us that Success is not always linear or easy. However, by learning from our experiences and staying committed to our goals, we can overcome obstacles and achieve our dreams.

Ultimately, *Winning Secrets* is a comprehensive guide to achieve Success across different aspects of life. Whether you're a business owner, an athlete, a student, or a self-motivated person striving for excellence, this book offers valuable insights and practical advice on how to achieve your goals and overcome obstacles along the way so you can consistently Win at life!

Winning Secrets is a must-read for anyone who is serious about achieving Success in their personal and professional life. It offers a wealth of valuable insights, practical advice, and inspiring stories that will motivate and guide readers towards their goals.

Whether you're just starting out on your journey or you're a seasoned pro, this book has something to offer.

Bottom line:

If you're ready to unlock the secrets of Winning at life and achieve your greatest potential, then *Winning Secrets* is the book for you!

Mr. Biz, aka Ken Wentworth

On-Demand CFO | Strategic Partner | Speaker | Author

Board Member | Radio Host | Investor

Introduction

Thank you for choosing to share some time with me. What you're about to read will literally change your life; it changed mine. Perhaps you're wondering who I am and how I'm Winning at life: "Why would someone I've never heard of, have the secrets to Winning?"

What really matters

That's a good question, and the answer is part of the greatest secret to Winning—it has absolutely nothing to do with me, with my achievements, with my net wealth, with my degrees or my education.

What I'm about to share with you will change your life forever **because** it has nothing to do with me. This Winning secret has everything to do with **you** and the fascinating, highly Successful people you'll meet in this book. Who we are and What we've accomplished has no impact whatsoever on your potential to Win and how you've *already Won*. And that's why this book is a must read.

Let's suppose that it's very important to you that the author of a book on Winning be super Successful. What are my credentials to prove that I know the secrets to Winning?

I don't have a huge house, I don't drive a Mercedes, I don't have seven figures in the bank, I'm not the highest-grossing salesman in my field, and there are people with more and higher degrees than me. For those people who have these things, I'm very happy for them....... if they are happy and fulfilled by these things.

In ways that deeply matter to me, I'm just like so many of you.

I'm grateful to be married to an incredible woman since 2003. There is no one I trust more; she has transformed my life in so many ways.

I have children who love me and are grateful for what I provide for them; they're hungry to learn and treasure our family experiences.

I'm part of a phenomenal company that combines a focus on the customer & employee experience with collaboration to create custom-tailored solutions that Elevate Businesses to Heroic Success.

I've had the privilege of serving my country in the United States and overseas in the Ohio Army National Guard.

Oh, and just like most of you, I put my pants on one leg at a time. I'm sure there are some overachievers out there that put on their pants *both legs* at the same time. And their pants are probably nicer too! Those overachievers!

One key reason why I wrote this book was to encourage so many people like me that, for far too long, have not given themselves the credit they deserve for all the Wins they **have** achieved.

I want to encourage you, inspire you, motivate you, and challenge you to achieve even more by sharing with you powerful tools that I'm using to do the same. And I have a host of respected Winners who agree with me that I'm on the right track.

I have a passion for writing. Through a great deal of positive feedback, I realized that I have an ability to write in a way that's enjoyable to read and easy to understand. What better way to use this gift than to share life-changing truths with others?

10 Keys to Win even more

Invest your time with me to discover the powerful, practical truths in this book, and I promise that you will be:

- Empowered to Win like never before
- Growing in healthy confidence
- Encouraged by your strong character and deeply held core values

- Motivated to reach for meaningful ambitions
- Inspired to achieve more than you thought possible
- Strengthened and equipped from your invaluable life experiences
- Tapped into the strongest sources of motivation & inspiration
- Freed to invest in rich, nourishing relationships
- Protected by establishing & enforcing boundaries
- Challenged to unleash one of the strongest forces in the universe

I've been there

Are you facing the most challenging time of your life?

When you look at others' lives, do they seem to have it all together? As if they know the magical secret to an easy, Successful life?

Why does it seem so hard to just keep up, let alone get ahead?

Does it feel like no matter how hard you try, you're still falling behind your peers?

Even while working two or three jobs, does one financial setback after another put you farther behind? Self-help books tell you to set goals or work harder or to believe in yourself, with advice like: "Start a side job", "Work for yourself", "Make your money work for you", "Save until it hurts" or "Just add another income". What do you tell yourself after you've done all those, and it *still* doesn't work?

In your quest for a better opportunity, how many times have you heard, "Great interview! But we've decided to go with someone else"? No matter how carefully you edit your resume or "dress for Success", the better opportunities just don't seem to come your way.

Do you feel like others are judging you, that they're assuming your life is so hard because of your poor choices? Even some people you thought were close friends are nowhere to be found when you have legitimate needs with no way to take care of them.

You're not alone. So many people have experienced this. I've been there. I know how this feels. If it weren't for loved ones depending on me, I may have been tempted to quit, to give up and settle for just staying alive, wishing I had achieved Success like everyone else around me.

But what if you're thinking, "That's not my story at all, John. My career is going well, I have lots of friends, I'm financially in good shape, and nothing is breaking down." Wonderful! I'm so glad to hear that your life is going smoothly. That was my life several years ago, just before our family experienced the most difficult years of our lives.

We've experienced times of plenty and times of need. We've had many people who called us friends, and times when we could count our true friends on only one hand. We've had times of being respected and trusted, as well as times when we were ignored and patronized.

Here's what I learned: **an easy life doesn't mean we're doing everything right, and a challenging life doesn't mean we're doing everything wrong.**

One big Winner you don't know

This book is about Winning and overcoming, and it starts with one, life-changing truth. So let me introduce someone to you.

Meet Trayvon Bromell. But before you Google him, let me share his achievements with you.

- He was the first junior sprinter to break the 10-second barrier for the 100-meter sprint.
- He was named the Gatorade Athlete of the Year for high school athletes in 2013.
- He missed setting the Baylor University record for the Men's 100-meter dash by only .01 seconds.
- He was the first freshman sprinter since Michael Johnson to be awarded the Texas Relay's Most Outstanding Performer.
- In the 2015 World Championships, he posted the tenth-fastest race of all time with a 9.84 second run.
- He beat out 30 other sprinters to qualify for one of the two coveted spots on the 2016 U.S. 100-meter Men's team.
- He ran faster than 62 of some of the fastest runners in the world to qualify for the Final 100-meter dash at the 2016 summer Olympics.
- At the 2021 Summer Olympics U.S. Trials, Trayvon won the top spot in the Men's 100-meter sprint.

"If he's such an accomplished athlete, why haven't we heard of him until the 2021 Olympic 100-meter dash final round?"—a reasonable question to ask. Here's why: one quarter of a second.   That's right—.25 seconds—the difference between being world-famous and practically unknown.

The setting for our story is the festive, South American metropolis of Rio de Janeiro, the summer of 2016. Usain Bolt Wins an unprecedented 3rd-straight gold medal in the Olympic Men's 100-meter dash. While cameras flash and the crowd roars, Bolt crosses the finish line first, by just one-tenth of a second ahead of the next-fastest sprinter. The whole world is amazed by the athletic feat of the 30-year-old sprinter from Jamaica. And rightly so.

Usain Bolt embodies the most common definition for Winning. He crossed the finish line first, and they placed the gold medal around his neck. He was the sole Winner in that race, right?

Wrong! Absolutely, totally wrong.

But before you think that I'm arguing with you (or insane!), please read just a little bit further. I would have been just as wrong about that perspective only a few years ago. What I discovered radically changed my entire perception of myself and others. My life has never been the same since.

What if I told you that your perception of yourself as a Winner is wrong?

What if I told you that your perception of others as Winners is also wrong?

In this book, I'm going to share transforming truths with you that will literally change your life. You'll never see your life in the same way again. Your view of yourself, and how you perceive those around you, will be transformed in a way you never thought possible.

Inspiration from the most unlikely place

Where did my enlightenment occur? In one of the least expected places—the dictionary. Before you think to yourself, "Oh gosh! Seriously? We're not going to have to read the dictionary, are we?!" Hang on. Much to the chagrin of dictionary readers across the world, we are **not** going to read Webster's dictionary. Let me share with you how my life changing "Aha Moments" happened.

At the beginning of 2017, I resolved to spend less time in front of a computer or TV and invest more time in reading to improve my personal and professional life.

Bill Gates, Warren Buffet, Oprah, Jeff Bezos, Elon Musk, Tony Robbins, Mark Zuckerberg, and Mark Cuban—are a few highly-Successful business leaders who promote reading books as a critical investment to enriching their lives. I took their advice, and I'm so glad I did!

My primary focus in my professional development reading was the topic of customer service. It's always been a top priority for me, in every career role. When I worked for companies that measured Customer Satisfaction, I was in the highest percentages every month.

New to Business-to-Business sales in 2017, my goal with my evening studies was to learn how to use my proven customer service skills to grow my employer's business in the Columbus, Ohio region. I proceeded to check out from the library or purchase from Amazon every well-rated book on excellent customer service to create ideas and connect them with sales growth.

As I studied industry leaders in customer service ratings, I was struck by a handful of key principles that were common to all of them, that had also served me well. First light bulb moment, "Bing!"

What if I could share with others a simple, individualized approach to improving their customer service? What if I added to that unique resource the ability to train entire teams with no inventory, no memorization, no scripts, and no new analytics? Best of all, what if I added a financial Thank You to every person who shared the resource with others?

Voila! The book *WOW Your Customers! 7 Ways to World-Class Service* was born. 18 months later, the website went live, and the book became available on Amazon.

Paradigm Shift

In order to be in the right frame of mind, I need to shake some things up for you. A paradigm shift is defined by Webster's as: "an important change that happens when the **usual way** of thinking about or doing something is replaced by a new and different way." (Emphasis added.)

Imagine that you were raised in the 1860's, when the Pony Express was created in America. Before this cutting-edge solution (at the time!), letters from the eastern United States to the west coast would take months to arrive by ship, requiring travel all the way around South America (there was no Panama Canal back then).

That would be your new normal. The Pony Express would be a vast improvement over sending and receiving mail by ship.

But what if you were suddenly dropped into 2020? The shocking difference between what was "normal" in 1860 and what is common today would be almost incomprehensible.

When I say that people, just like you and me, are Winning every single day, that seems to fly in the face of reality. That seems to be impossible...but only because of what we've come to believe is "normal."

Forget "normal." Forget "common knowledge."

Embrace the life-changing, legitimate paradigm shifts I will share with you in the following pages.

Why? It would be tragic if you lived the rest of your life thinking that the Pony Express is the best communication method the world will ever get, when live video conferences with professionals on the other side of the world are available to you.

I'm asking you to trust me. Take a little time with me and hear me out. You'll be glad you did!

Where my Paradigm Shift began

The very first chapter of my book on customer service began with what I believe is an absolute necessity to bring enthusiastic, engaging service to every customer—a Winning attitude.

As I was writing one evening, it suddenly struck me: what was the actual definition for Winning? I had never looked up that word before; I had always assumed that Winning was coming in first, beating everyone else in a competition.

So I pulled out my red, hardcover Webster's dictionary from my college days. The first definition for "Winning" was exactly what I suspected: "relating to or producing a Win." Coming in first—no surprise there.

It was the second definition that literally brought the world to a stop for me. And that was my second "Aha Moment."

If you've read my book, *WOW Your Customers! 7 Ways to World-Class Service*, then you already know the definition. For those of you who have not had the pleasure of reading my book (yet).... find out in the very next chapter how just one word changed my entire view on life.

Chapter 1

What and Whose

"Everybody is a genius. But if you judge a fish by its ability to climb a tree, it will live its whole life thinking it is stupid."
--Albert Einstein

I almost stopped breathing for a moment when I read the one-word definition for "Winning." It was in all-caps, practically leaping off the page at me. When I read it, one incredible insight after another hit me:

- If our definition of Winning at life is wrong, then the majority of our life may be sadly chalked up as a loss.
- How we determine a "Win" or a "loss" in life is based on the wrong criteria.
- The vast majority of people in the world are Winners, and they don't even realize it.

Winning Secret #1—What It Is—The Right Definition

I promised you at the end of the last chapter that I'd share with you Webster's second definition for Winning, so here it is:

SUCCESS.

If fireworks did not go off in your brain or you feel extremely underwhelmed by this one word, hang in there with me! I can absolutely guarantee your life will be dramatically changed as we unpack this incredible, life-changing secret. Here's why this one word matters so much.

Boiled down to its essence, Success is simply defined as what worked. Did it work? That's Success. Did it fail? Believe it or not, that also leads to Success. That's right— Success or failure—**both** are a part of Winning, but only when you apply the correct definition **and** the correct measure. To prove to you that I am **not** enjoying the legal use of psychedelic mushrooms in my own home, let me share some examples with you!

Who said this: "I've failed over and over and over again in my life, and that is why I succeed." Or "I have not failed. I've just found 10,000 ways that don't work." Or number 3: "Failure is Success in progress." What if I told you that all three of these people are known around the world as highly Successful? The three people are Michael Jordan, Thomas Edison, and Albert Einstein.

In 2015, Tiffany High took decisive action. She wanted to make a difference in the Toledo, Ohio area by pursuing her passion in real estate investment to change peoples' lives. When I spoke with Tiffany, she credited failure as one of the key reasons for her massive, fast-growing Success.

"I learned the hard way more than once," she shared. "At first, it was difficult to realize that my unsuccessful choices resulted in significant financial losses. But we learned what not to do, continuously improved, and sought advice & counsel from experienced mentors in our field." The results have been impressive, to say the least.

As of the writing of this book, Tiffany, her husband Josh, and the rock star team at Results Driven, are on pace to earn over $4 million in revenue and are equipping real estate investors with the same tools and processes to grow their portfolios. Check out the great work her team and her husband, Josh, are doing on their website: www.tiffanyandjoshhigh.com.

Failures can be our greatest asset to achieving our dreams, especially when we categorize them as invaluable learning experiences on our path to accomplishing our life goals.

During a client visit a few years ago, I noticed an intriguing plaque hung on the wall next to their whiteboard. The 6-word quote simply stated: "Progress is the goal, not perfection."

If our definition of Winning is perfection, we will never consider ourselves to have Won until we reach some remarkable milestone. Even worse, we will not see ourselves as Winners *right now*.

Our lives are chock full of Wins, and we don't even realize it. No matter what your present circumstances are in life, the truth is that you're Winning far, far more than losing. To better explain how this is true, let me ask you a few questions:

- Can a football team lose a game, yet a player still Win?
- Can a student have a lower grade than their classmates, yet still Win?
- Can a child mature more slowly than their siblings, yet still Win?
- Can an employee master their tasks at a slower pace than their co-workers, and still Win?

- Can an actor be passed over for the leading role of a blockbuster film, and still Win?
- Can a salesperson earn less of a bonus than their counterparts, and still Win?
- Can a company serve fewer customers than their neighboring businesses, and still Win?
- Can a realtor care for new homebuyers with fewer houses sold than their team members, and still Win?

The answer to all these questions is a resounding "Yes!", when you have the correct definition for Winning—Success.

Compared to what?

As of 2022, Warren Buffet's estimated net worth was under $98 billion. Just to put that into perspective, $1 billion in $1 dollar bills, laid end to end, would circle the globe four times. That's just $1 billion; Mr. Buffet has almost 100 times that!

Financial advisors recommend a retirement account that has a minimum of $1 million invested by the time you are ready to start the next chapter of your life. That string of

$1 bills stretches just 100 miles, about the distance from Columbus, Ohio to Cincinnati, Ohio. Wow! That's an enormous difference between Warren Buffet's net worth and a Successful retiree's account balance. But it's still not the most alarming comparison.

Do you know what the average 50-year-old American has saved for retirement? According to Northwestern Mutual, the average investment account in 2018 held about $180,000. That string of dollar bills that only makes it 17 miles down the road—about the width of the city of Columbus, Ohio.

Here's my point. Compared to Mr. Buffet's Success, a retiree who accumulates a wise amount of investment funds could appear to be a loser. Yet, when compared to the average investment account, that retiree is astronomically ahead, clearly a Winner. And even the average investor is still much further ahead of the one who has nothing set aside. In each situation, the investor needs to determine what Winning financially looks like to them, not to others.

Winning Secret #2—The Right Ruler

That's the second Winning Key: the one best definition for Winning is *your* Success.

You define your Success, not someone else.

Now let's go back to the story in the introduction, to Trayvon Bromell.

In the 2016 Olympic Men's 100-meter dash final, the race that Usain Bolt completed first, Trayvon came across the line dead last—.25 seconds after Usain. When you apply the second Winning Secret of Success as the definition for Winning, Trayvon won so many times just to qualify for that final sprint.

We would all agree that when an athlete is elected to the Hall of Fame of their respective sport, that they have been recognized as an exceptional athlete, as a Winner. So let me throw some NFL names at you:

- Andre Reed
- Jim Kelly
- Steve Tasker
- Darryl Talley
- Bruce Smith
- Phil Hansen
- Thurman Thomas

These men are all in the National Football Hall of Fame in Canton, Ohio. All 7 of these top athletes achieved a record that no other players have to date: 4 straight Super Bowl appearances.

And yet, when I did a recent search on Google, the very first headline said that team was "overrated." How can historic be overrated?!

Because the Buffalo Bills did not Win the Super Bowl in those 4 appearances.

Unless a person has played in the NFL, they cannot fully comprehend the endurance, sacrifice, and effort it takes to make it to the Super Bowl once, let alone four times. But because these 7 players do not have a Super Bowl championship ring on their finger, these men and their historic teams are not considered by others to be Winners.

That's why most reporters' questions at the Olympics or the Super Bowl or the World Cup, or any major sporting event, bother me so much. Rather than asking an athlete, coach or team what they're proud of achieving, they almost always ask how they feel about losing if they do not come in first. This question is completely wrong because it assumes that the world-class athlete or team did not Win. They're already defining their efforts as a loss.

Don't let others decide if you're succeeding or if you're Winning.

I did the same thing to myself for most of my life, so please get this! **Those athletes had hundreds, if not thousands, of Wins to place themselves in the opportunity to Win the ultimate prize.** Trayvon was one of the eight fastest sprinters in the world in Rio!!

Win after Win after Win while he was training, preparing, competing, eating, healing, and learning---all enabled him to get to the 2016 Olympics.

One wise investment after another earned Warren Buffet a place in life where he is recognized for his lucrative investments.

One victory after another for the Buffalo Bills earned them a spot in the Super Bowl—four years in a row.

Your life has been full of Wins every single day, resulting in the Success you have experienced and the Successes still ahead. Please remember that Winning is Success—what works.

- Did you wake up, get up, and head to work or school?
- Did you safely drive to your first destination?
- Did you take care of your loved ones?

- Did your efforts contribute positively to society?
- Did you do your job to the best of your ability?

Your faithful devotion to what works, to Successful choices, has brought you to a place in your life where you're so much farther ahead than when you were younger. And it will always lead to greater Success. John Maxwell rightly said, "Success is not a destination thing; it is a daily thing."

But even with the correct definition of Winning— Success—if your measurement of Success is someone else's, you're confining yourself to the results of someone else's efforts, someone else's achievements. You're allowing someone else to determine your level of Success.

Take a moment, right now, before we move on to the next Winning Secret, to take stock of the Wins you already have. You'll be so encouraged by applying this life-changing definition for Winning—the many Successes in life you've already achieved.

(For real.....stop reading and make a list of all the Successes you have achieved in your life, no matter your age or where you are currently in life, education, or career. Do.It.Now!!)

Archaeology and Winning

It sounds like the beginning of a joke: A German curator walks into a Turkish museum... In 1916, Eckhard Unger, curator of the Archaeological Museum of Istanbul identified a copper-like object as an Assyrian measuring device, dating back to 2500 BC. It was the oldest-known, hand-crafted device to consistently measure length, in this case, the Sumerian cubit. We commonly refer to this tool as the ruler.

A few years ago, I went to the store that begins with "Wal" and ends in "mart" and bought myself a bright-blue, shiny metal ruler. I keep it right above my desk as a visual reminder of an invaluable Winning Secret. Before I explain why I bought the ruler, think about why we use them for a moment.

Measurement is a good thing—it gives us a standard to determine accuracy. My favorite number is 7. How intriguing that writing a book on Winning at Life would uncover that there are 7 types of measurement!

1. Length
2. Time
3. Mass
4. Electrical current
5. Temperature
6. Light intensity
7. Substance

Imagine a world without a ruler, without these 7 standards, without measurements.

- How do you build a strong, safe house without using the same foot or inch?
- How would we ever arrive for a meeting at the same time if our minute is different from our co-worker's minute?
- How would we know that there are 20 ounces of water in our bottle every time we purchased a 24-pack from the store?
- How would we know that our home is getting enough power to run all our appliances?
- How would we know if today is warmer than yesterday?
- How would we know which light bulb to buy if 100 watts has less light than 25 watts?

- How horribly different (and unsafe!) would everyday objects like roads, buildings, maps, bridges, automobiles, ships, planes, trains, or tunnels be?
- How impossible would it be to complete detailed procedures like carpentry, mathematics, or surgery?!

Measurement is a wonderful process that enables precision, quality, innovation, and strength. But life doesn't work that way, not at all!

Winner take all?

Our experiences in life do not come with such precise standards of measurement. To add to the confusion, many people believe that Winning is an all-or-nothing deal, a zero-sum game where only one team gets the championship trophy at the end of the season, only one business has the highest sales in a year, only one class member has the highest GPA, only one actor has the highest-grossing film of the year, etc.

As children, we may have felt like we could never measure up to the high expectations our well-intended parents had for us or the challenging ones we had for ourselves. Without realizing it, parents, schools, sports programs, businesses, leaders, and especially ourselves, have all contributed to so many people feeling inadequate, less than others or as losers.

As a father, trainer, manager, businessman, sports enthusiast, and well-meaning self-critic, I fit all these categories, until I realized that I had the wrong unit of measure. My life-changing insight came from changing just two letters—"st."

For all those years, I had the wrong word tense. I strove to be the fast**est**, smart**est**, and rich**est** of my peers. I wanted to be the mo**st** trusted, mo**st** well-liked, and the mo**st** respected. And what happened when I realized that I was not?

One of two things—a) denial, with more fruitless efforts, or b) giving up, resigning myself to failure in these pursuits. Neither way is healthy, and neither way is actually attainable. Worst of all, neither way is true of us.

Just two little letters

Change those two letters, and you've got it: change "**st**" to "**r**", and "**st**" to "**re**". "Faste**r**", "smarte**r**", "riche**r**" and "mo**re** trusted", "mo**re** well-liked", and "mo**re** respected."

I'm not talking about participation trophies where everybody gets one.

I'm not talking about satisfactory or unsatisfactory performance where quality doesn't matter.

We'll address the need for a coachable attitude and a willingness to improve later. We must shift our paradigm first so that we start with the correct definitions for Winning, for Success.

What's most important to understand here, is this:

Use your own measuring stick of Success, not someone else's.

Unless you are measuring your present self to your former self, your perception of your Wins, compared to others, will almost always look like that of a loser. There will always be someone who has done more, earned more, achieved more, than you.

Warren Buffet is not the wealthiest man in the world. And there are faster sprinters than Trayvon Bromell. But they would both be considered highly Successful—when using the right measuring stick—for what they have achieved in their life...*compared to where they started.* Warren Buffet wasn't born with a billion dollars in his crib, and Trayvon didn't start out as the fastest sprinter at his Texas preschool.

It was their journey and the choices along the way that enabled them to Win, to succeed at a very high level. Just as it was for Michael Jordan, Thomas Edison, and Albert Einstein. This leads us to the next powerful insight.

Whose ruler are you using?

Don't be like me, the "old John", who thought: "I'll never be as Successful as those people." Forget about those people! My thought should have been: "I am more Successful today than I was last year, two years ago, five years ago."

Think back to when you first became an adult: aren't you clearly more Successful now than at that time of your life?! Always remember:

The best standard of measure is the Present You compared to the Past You.

"But, John, nothing is working in my life right now," you may be thinking. Our family struggled through under-employment for several years; I know exactly how you feel.

This is why we must embrace the best definition for Winning—our Successes with the correct ruler—the Present us versus the Past us.

Our Success in life is not fully dependent on our circumstances.

Our life experiences will ebb and flow with levels of Success, achievement, and income throughout our life—sometimes, life will be pleasant, and sometimes, life will be difficult.

Our time in life can affect how we perceive our Success. As a teenager and a student, I did not have many life experiences to learn from as I do now in my forties. My perception of Success would have been based primarily upon my schooling, personal relationships, and hobbies or interests.

College students often do not have workplace experience to evaluate their growth, so their determination of Success is often focused on their GPA, graduation date, or career prospects.

Full-time mothers, who have chosen to pause their careers to invest into their children, have a unique challenge in measuring Success because nurturing children is a long-term effort that takes many years to result in mature, productive, happy adults.

We cannot base our Winning at life by comparing our current situation with other people or their apparent level of Success or happiness. Here are two major reasons why, our next two Winning Secrets.

Others' Success is an illusion

I encourage you to read the book, *The Millionaire Next Door* by Thomas J. Stanley & William Danko. When I was completing my business degree, one of my papers included a study based on their findings.

The greatest takeaway for me was the difference between actual millionaires—those whose net worth exceeded $10 million—and high wage-earners. One group owned $10 million or more in assets, while the other group **appeared** to have $10 million or more. The startling truth was that high wage-earners were just as much paycheck to paycheck as our family was when we were under-employed!

Finances aren't the only way that we can inaccurately measure Success. How many families or marriages appear to have it all together, yet years later, major issues are discovered?

The truth is we do not know what challenges others are going through until we are intimately involved in their lives on a daily basis. That's when we find out what is actually going on in their life compared to what we *perceive* is going on in their life.

Reality versus perception.

Throughout this chapter, we've seen how comparison can be a helpful tool or a dangerous illusion. We must use this wisely and not rely on our perception of others or their perception of us. Let me explain.

It's often a case of Recognition versus Reality. It's not about how many people recognize the repeated Successes we have in our lives, the Winning.

It doesn't matter if there are billions who identify us as Winners or Successful, or hundreds of people, or ten people.

The reality is that the vast majority of us are Winning every day.

Winning is a very active word. Winning doesn't come to people who are lucky, and it doesn't magically fall to people out of the sky. It comes from hard work that persists to overcome challenges, limited time, the doubts of others, financial hurdles, expectations—conquering one hurdle after another.

In some people's minds, Successful always equals more. More than last month, more than last year, etc. But if Success, the actual definition and reality of it, is being achieved, then people can be discouraged if the measurable results now are less than what they experienced before. But does that mean that person is not Successful, that they're not Winning?

I believe that most often the misapplication of the word Success is caused by external forces or vague expectations, either from a system or from leaders & authority figures in our lives.

For example, if a student gets straight-A grades one year, and the next year gets all A's and one B, was the student unsuccessful? Their GPA would undoubtedly be an A average, but if you take the misapplication of Success, that student would most likely be labeled with an unsuccessful year. Despite all the work, all the effort, all the studying, all the dedication to achieve all those A's and just one B, because their GPA was a little bit less than last year's, they would be labeled as having an unsuccessful year.

That's a tragedy. And it happens in so many peoples' lives--at work, in school, in relationships, while chasing our dreams.

Our Success must be measured in every aspect of our life in order to be real. By only looking at one aspect of our lives—most likely the one that didn't meet our goals or expectations—what we end up doing is labeling ourselves as losers, when the reality is exactly the opposite—we are overwhelmingly Winning.

Let's revisit the example of Trayvon versus Usain. Billions of people recognize Usain Bolt as a Winner, and rightly so.

But what about the other seven runners in all those races that Usain Bolt won? They were all highly accomplished Winners. They were amongst a group of the eight fastest sprinters in the world! But the other seven runners were labeled as losers because they didn't have the gold medal, the fastest time, the first place on the podium.

Life, in a wonderful way, does not work that way. We can all succeed, we can all Win, **without others losing**.

That's the beauty of applying this to our lives first, before factoring in the expectations of ourselves and others. We could end up causing great damage to ourselves, our loved ones, our team, our neighbors, if we don't start first with the entire reality of what they are achieving.

Except for those individuals who are committed to a life of wrong choices, everyone is seeking to achieve something. And who am I to say that what they are trying to achieve means less than what I am trying to achieve? Shame on me for the times that I have taken my expectations, my goals, my dreams, my priorities and applied them to others' lives.

Getting to a depth of relationship to know others' finances, strength of relationships, goals, and dreams is extremely rare.

The only reality we can ever fully know is our own.

And our reality is our present state, not our past or our future state. Our reality can absolutely be changed by our choices...which leads me to the second reason to base our measure of Success on ourselves.

It's their ruler, not ours

Remember my bright-blue, shiny metal ruler? This visual reminder is in my office where I see it every day. I need to be reminded of this Winning insight often. As I observe others' lives, I see brand-new cars, beautiful houses, nicely dressed couples enjoying an expensive dinner, happy shoppers leaving stores with large bags of purchases, and sharp businesspeople in expensive suits with multiple awards on their desks.

If their ruler was my measure of Success, how disappointed would I be with my reality? How unreasonably hard would I push myself to achieve more, to be more like them? How unhappy would I be to never reach my *perception* of others' Success?

Especially on those days when I'm tempted to be discouraged, I think about my $1.99 bright-blue, shiny metal ruler and tell myself, "Not your ruler, John. That's not your measurement of Success."

Do not become a slave to what you **think** others' happiness is, when they may be searching for the exact same thing you are. You would be surprised by how many of them are unsatisfied with where they are and where they want to be.

But what about results that can be measured and are used as a comparison between us and others in the same role? This is common in fields like business, sports, education, and the military.

Competition can be a strong motivator to spur us on to achieve more. It's been proven that horses racing against each other result in faster run times than if a steed circled the track on its own. The challenge of seven other sprinters in the blocks next to Trayvon Bromell infused him with adrenaline and a strong desire to run faster. These are positive motivators.

The danger of competition happens when our results are not the highest, the fastest, or the most. The simple and common conclusion is that because we were not Number One that we lost. While it is true that there can only be one person or team that comes in first...

There is always more than one Winner.

Now worth an estimated $3 billion, Oprah Winfrey said in a 2001 interview that one of her keys to having wealth was to "not let wealth use you, but you use it. Being a person who has come from an outhouse, and very poor circumstances, I can assure you that the more money you get, it really doesn't change you—unless you are the kind of person who is defined by money."

And there is the key freeing principle:

WE must define our Success rather than have it, or our perception of it, define us.

Winning Secret #3: The Right Celebrations-- Compound Progress

Do you know what the smallest unit of measure is on my bright-blue, shiny metal ruler? One millimeter. Think back to that sign I saw at a business partner of ours: "Progress is the goal, not perfection."

Mark Twain said that continued improvement is better than delayed perfection. That is the heart of genuine, Win/Win continuous improvement: "How can we do this better?" It's not glamorous or fun, but the daily grind of diligent perseverance results in a lifetime of major achievements. One million millimeters add up to over half a mile! Our right choices add up to progressive Success.

John Maxwell said, "Doing the right thing daily, compounds over time." Right choices over time always add up to Winning more at life.

It was Albert Einstein who said that compound interest is the 8th wonder of the world, the strongest force in the universe. Just like compound interest builds money upon itself, Compound Progress works by building future Successes upon the previous ones.

There's an enormous difference in one key way between Compound Progress and compound interest: money invested can sit for decades and grow with someone else's oversight. Compound Progress is all you!

That's why the opposite of progress in Winning is not failure, but stagnation—giving up. No movement either way.

Those who are fail*ing* are still try*ing*. The ones who have given up will never have the opportunity to succeed.

Not all of Warren Buffet's investments have been Successful, so he learned from those experiences and used those lessons as insight for his future investments. Trayvon did not Win every single sprint; he used his losses to drive him to keep working hard while learning how to run faster.

Failures are a gigantic advantage to those determined to build on them. Steve Allen, co-founder of Microsoft, said: "In my experience, each failure contains the seeds of your next Success—if you are willing to learn from it."

Remember how we said that failure is a part of Success? It absolutely is, when we use it to continuously improve, to leverage the lessons learned in future decisions.

We've made a strong case to support the fact that we're already Winning.

You are a Winner; you are highly Successful.

So the logical question is: how do we Win more?

Great question! That's what we will explore in the chapters to follow, unlocking 8 proven secrets to a fulfilling life, to Winning more.

Ruler of our own Destiny

Quick question for you: when you hear the word "Destiny", what do you think of? The actual definition will surprise you! A common saying is that each of us is the Ruler of our own Destiny. This is what used to come to my mind:

"Luke, it is your destiny [with heavy breathing through a black mask]." Or a wrinkle-faced old man in desperate need of skin lotion cackling about the good guys losing one star fighter after another?

Yes, I'm a huge fan of *Star Wars*, ever since I was a kid and saw it for the first time in my friend's basement. Do you remember statements like, "I have foreseen it...it is your destiny"? The bad guys were trying to convince Luke Skywalker that he was destined to be a bad guy. Was he? Did he just go along with their opinion of what his destiny was supposed to be? He absolutely did not, and that's why he is a beloved character.

Destiny is not a force outside of us or dependent upon someone else's definition, just like Winning. So what is the real definition for destiny?

It comes from the Latin word *destinare*, meaning to determine or intend. It's where we get the word "Destination." Destiny is not some magical, mystical hope of where we wish to be sometime in the future or what will ultimately happen to us no matter what actions we take. Not at all!

Destiny is the result of an intentional, unwavering pursuit of what we have determined to achieve.

Our Destiny is not determined by anything or anyone outside of ourselves. That's why cloning humans will never result in the exact same human being. They can clone our physical attributes, but they cannot clone our collective decisions that result in a uniquely individual journey called Life.

We are all human be-ings, not human been's. We are living out our humanness, and how we choose to live results in the people we become—our Destiny.

Change your ruler, change your Destiny.

You determine how you measure Winning and where you want it to take you. Destiny has nothing to do with Hoping; it has everything to do with Honing.

Now that this amazing new paradigm shift has empowered you to Win on a whole new level, let's explore the next important step to experiencing a fulfilling life— discovering Who You Are as you work to fulfill your Destiny.

Winning Secrets—What & Whose

- What it is—SUCCESS!
  - Not just coming in first
- The best definition for Success is *your Success*
  - You define it, not others
- Whose ruler are you using?
  - Measure your progress with your Past You
- Others' Success is an illusion
  - Our own reality--the only one we fully know
- It's their ruler, not ours
  - Remind ourselves of this daily
- Compound Progress
  - Build on one Success & failure after another
- Rulers of our own Destiny
  - Work rather than wish

Winning Secrets: The Right Definition, The Right Ruler & The Right Celebrations

My Menu

_____

_____

_____

_____

_____

_____

Chapter 2

Who Are You?

"What is necessary to change a person

is to change his awareness of himself."

Abraham Maslow

Who are you? That would be an awesome name for a song, maybe even a band! [Quick Google search for song titled "Who Are You?"]. Dang it! [Another quick Google search for a band called "Who"]. Darn it!! It would've been an even better idea if I had thought of these before I was born!

As silly as this sounds, we do this to ourselves. We need to stop blaming ourselves for something we could never be: someone else.

Along with a fresh definition for Winning, a realization of how uniquely special we are, is critical to having a fulfilled life. Even more important—we must realize that we were created to Win. We were meant to have purpose, and that automatically includes Success, what works, Winning at life.

The purpose of this chapter is to encourage you, to help you realize the incredible potential and tailored giftedness that applies only to you. I'm not talking about feel-good sentiment or psychological mind tricks to make you feel better about yourself. This entire book is devoted to reality, what is actually true.

As we work through this chapter, be honest and vulnerable with yourself. Commit to gathering feedback from people you trust—mentors, coaches, close friends, respected colleagues, appreciative customers, etc. By the end of this chapter, my goal is for you to be empowered with a new awareness of your astounding capabilities and reinforce these newfound insights with constructive truth from people you trust.

Identity

Who we are is far more than just our name. There are two definitions from Webster's that I'll quickly share with you. The first describes identity as "the distinguishing character or personality of an individual." We'll touch on this definition as we walk through this chapter, but listen to the second description.

"The condition of being the same as something described or asserted." It may sound like this applies to an inanimate object rather than a person, but let's look at it again by meeting two extraordinary people.

Purpose discovered at 70!

Imagine being abused as a child, both physically and verbally, being called names like "worthless", "trash", "stupid", "useless", "dog", and "curse of the family." It's not surprising that this person wrestled with depression, anxiety, loss, fear, and doubt. They experienced health issues, loss of children, and a fruitless search for spiritual healing. But that's not how the story ends!

In the spring of 2019, I had the privilege of meeting Pat Gano, the person I just shared with you. Before I dive into her story, I highly recommend that you buy her book, *The Language of Heaven: 5 Gifts that Create Legacy,* on Amazon. It's an uplifting, encouraging read that will help heal deep and painful personal wounds from childhood.

As I read Pat's book, I felt so heavy and sad; how tragic for a child to be so heavily damaged by the ones who should have loved her the most. What a challenge for her to overcome such hurtful lies and slander.

Half-truths are very dangerous, not because of the lies, but *because of the truths that seem to validate the lies.*

This dear, sweet woman shared her story with me. After struggling most of her life from the pain of her childhood, Pat awoke one night with a clear calling for her life. The cool part? She was 70 years old at the time! I met her when she was 85. By that time, she had written her first book at 84, and shared her 10-year vision with me. This lady is an inspiration. Another proof that age is just a number!

In her mind, for most of her life, her identity was what people asserted, or told her, that it was. Those terrible, damaging words and experiences affected Pat for decades, because she thought they were true of her.

Because of the negative impact this had on her life, Pat is committed to investing into the lives of others so that they can experience decades of freedom and purpose, adding value to others. But her story was not unique, I discovered.

Loss of a father at 8 years old

At 6 years old, John watched his strong, 6'4", 250-pound father wither away to 160 pounds, requiring assistance for even basic life functions, during his 2-year bout with cancer. At 8 years old, John no longer had a father.

Not knowing how to deal with the grief and loss in such a traumatic time, John's life decisions reflected the hurt and pain he was feeling inside. His grades plummeted to D's and F's, his circle of friends was filled with negative influences, his relationship with his girlfriend remained despite her repeated infidelity, and the music he listened to elevated poor life choices and values. At one point, John was told by a teacher that he would never amount to anything.

The man I sat across from in the coffee shop is bright, articulate, professional, compassionate, and well-spoken. Obviously, what his teacher told him was a lie. But his grades and life choices were awful as a young man—the truth that supposedly validated the lie.

Today, Dr. John Tyus has committed his life to pouring into young men who do not have fathers in their lives. He not only turned his life around; his passion is to spare young men from the negative lack of purpose he experienced. Check out his mission on Facebook at The I.D. Movement; you'll be inspired!

Self-Love

So what enabled Pat and John to overcome the cruel lies and vicious labels that others asserted was true of them?

Realizing their reason for being, our greatest identity.

We were all created with the capacity to love and a strong desire to be loved. I used to think that self-love sounded creepy or selfish. But I was wrong. It's not what you're thinking it is. It's actually not about ourselves at all.

Self-Love is not loving ourselves. Self-Love is embracing the truth that we are loved more than we can fathom and that we deserve to be loved. We were created with the unquenchable desire to be loved.

Our purpose for being, at our very core, is all about love. Even if the physical act that began our lives was devoid of love, our gestation, birth, and care as a child, all required love. Love is far more than an emotion.

Our love is demonstrated most clearly by what we do.

The people who have the hardest time showing love to others most likely suffered from a severe lack of it as a child, but they were loved more than they realize by something outside of their upbringing.

To grasp how much we are loved, we must look beyond the human element. The very miracle of our lives, the fact that you and I not only exist, but are experiencing life in all of its fullness, is one of the strongest examples of divine love. Just take a moment to consider the staggering science behind the wonder of your life:

- Your life began the moment your mother was conceived
  - You were one of millions of eggs
- One sperm fertilized your egg—one out of many millions
- 50/50 chance that your fertilized egg would develop
- Heartbeat—8 weeks
  - No beating heart, no life
- Hearing—5 months
  - Inner ear connected correctly? We can hear!
- Sight—6 months

- Our eye nerves grow ***towards each other***. Only perfect alignment results in eyesight. Wow!
  - Brain development begins—6 months
    - The most complex supercomputer ever!
  - Birth—9 months
    - One of the most powerful human experiences

We take ourselves for granted far too often! In the process of human development, so many things had to go exactly right for us to have life, a heartbeat, hearing, eyesight, full brain function, and life outside of the womb. Remarkable! You are an incredibly unique masterpiece— **that is a fact!!**

But the miracle of life does not stop with birth. Think for a moment about your childhood.

I have fallen more times than I can count, been kicked in the face by a horse, knocked out my own front tooth with my knee, sprained my ankles several times, just to name a few! I persevered to complete basic training in Georgia during the summer with a unit composed mostly of soldiers half my age. I had the privilege of serving my country by deploying to Iraq in 2010 to protect our soldiers and allies in our bases from rocket and mortar attacks.

My children have been spared from multiple near-misses that could have ended their lives—adventures that included climbing a 50-foot pine tree in sock feet as a 4 year-old, inserting screwdrivers into empty, *wired* light bulb sockets, petting a momma horse with her young foal right next to her, and walking through the woods for half a mile to visit Daddy...without Mommy knowing they left! Yanking our kids back as they are just about to dash across the street or the parking lot to have a car whiz by, narrowly missing them.

Some of my friends reflect with wonder that they survived their childhood! The stories I've heard about things they should've never done that seemed, well, totally normal to the mind of an adventurous child. I mean, who doesn't jump off the roof with a sheet for a parachute? All superheroes started as little boys and girls, didn't they?

And those "interesting" teenage years or the first years behind the wheel as a new driver. If you stop for a moment to consider all the close calls you can remember, and those you are blissfully unaware of, your life is a constantly unfolding miracle.

"Okay, okay, John. I get your point. My life is a miracle. But I don't feel miraculous." Are you thinking this to yourself right now? Odds are, most of you reading this book feel this way about yourselves.

Part of this is because most of us are naturally modest—we do not want to think too much of ourselves. This tendency towards humility is a very good quality. So please do me a favor: for the rest of this chapter, set aside your reserved nature and allow me to share powerful truths with you to encourage you in positive reality.

There are dark, dangerous, and damaging secrets that directly contribute to our hesitancy to love ourselves, so we need to bring these things to the light.

Self-Esteem

When I was single, my younger brother and I shared an apartment. While flipping through the TV channels, we would occasionally settle on a public television program called *The Antiques Roadshow*. People would be filmed at an antiques convention while bringing their items to experienced appraisers to determine their potential value. Sometimes, the appraiser would value the item lower than the owner's estimate, so they would seek out a second opinion. Other times, the owner would be so excited, blown away that their old, scuffed teacup was a Victorian-era relic worth many thousands of dollars. There are two powerful principles about self-esteem here.

For antique owners that believed their item was worth more than the appraiser's opinion, what did they have to base that on? They were not the experts and did not have experience like the appraiser. Most often, it was because they had seen similar items appraised for more or they simply believed that it held more value than the expert said.

Here's the first principle on self-esteem: ultimately, the value we see in ourselves is most important, not the value others' see in us. Whether we under-value, over-value or accurately assess our worth, what we believe to be true carries the most weight.

Here's why. Our minds are incredibly powerful computers. What we put in them will directly affect what we experience in our lives. Our belief shapes our actions and prepares us to look for circumstances that affirm our beliefs. Let me give you an example.

When I began driving a bright blue Dodge Dart, I noticed other Dodge Darts on the road. Those cars were there before, but I was not aware of them because I was not sitting behind the wheel of a Dodge Dart. (No, Dodge is NOT sponsoring this book!)

Similarly, if we believe that we are of little worth, we will be looking for things in our lives that prove this to be true.

Because of the terrible lies they were told, Pat and John believed that they had little or no value. And as their lives unfolded, their experiences continued to affirm that they were not valuable or adding value to themselves and others.

Until they were able to attack and refute the lies that they had believed for far too long, Pat and John were not freed to add value to others. Here is another key for us, **Winning Secret #4**:

You cannot add value to others if you do not realize how valuable you are. *You cannot give away what you do not possess.*

Going back to the Antiques Roadshow example, what about the times when owners were shocked by the appraised value? In our personal lives, this occurs when influential people not only recognize our potential but reveal it to us and encourage us to pursue our dreams, living up to our potential.

We'll expand on this critically important piece in Winning more in the 6th chapter. For now, understand that it is more important to listen to the "expert" in your life that encourages you to achieve your full potential rather than believing you have little to offer.

Just because one appraiser said the antique teacup was of little value, did not mean that another appraiser would agree. Webster's dictionary defines esteem as: the regard in which something is held. It's subjective!! It is truly in the eye of the beholder.

If we're alive, we have unlimited potential. I've met more and more people in their 70's or older with incredible purpose and a strong vision for their lives. I've worked alongside people with physical challenges that were intelligent assets to the team. I've met young people totally passionate about adding value to others' lives. I know young people who are already financially secure, long before I was even thinking about my financial future.

So do me a favor, right now. As painful as this may be, write down all the mean, cruel, hurtful, slanderous things that anyone has ever said to you. It doesn't matter if those words described your life at the time or were complete lies; write every single one down on a sheet of paper.

Do It Now: write down with a pen & paper every mean, cruel, hurtful thing anyone has said to you.

One of our sons' coaches had a mantra he repeated incessantly during practice: Do It Now. He told our boys to apply this slogan to their lives outside of sports, too. If they were given a task, Do It Now.

Throughout this book, you will see Do It Now, followed by an exercise. Please do what Coach Forman said: Do It Now. Don't put it off; don't keep reading. Do. It. Now. You'll be glad you did, I promise.

Did you do it? For real......please take just a moment to jot down these half-truths and full-blown lies. It's important.

After you've made that list, cross out every single one and write next to them what caring people have said to you that is the exact opposite. You need to believe the positive, encouraging people who realize your incredible potential. Write their name and what they said about you that was affirming and positive.

Do It Now: write down every kind, affirming thing people have said to you, along with their names on the same sheet of paper, after crossing out the mean, hurtful things others have said.

Don't rush through this exercise; you may be facing decades of half-truths, lies, and heartache. See my example below.

Hurtful words	Positive Words	Who said them
~~Too old for new career~~	Glad to have you	Todd
~~Farmer, not a hunter~~	Invaluable asset	John
~~Terrible speaker~~	Excellent teacher	Jason

Did you do it? In order for this Winning tool to have the most impact personally, you really need to dig deep, go way back in your life. Not only will this help affirm your worth and potential, it will also begin the process of healing.

Those kind, affirming, specific words that caring people shared with you? THAT is the truth!

We need to recognize the bitter, hateful lies of hurting, angry people for the hot, nasty, steaming piles of manure that they are. No matter what sliver of truth is included, they are lies. Most often, the truths are what happened to us, or others' polluted opinions, **not Who we actually are**. During our conversation, John Tyus shared a powerful analogy with me, so let me share it with you now.

Self-Care

You are loved, and you are valuable.

Those are facts, truths that you must affirm daily, especially when certain events trigger memories of past hurts and lies. There's a practical step we must take after realizing these truths in order to have the energy to boldly claim them every day—self-care.

John shared that we should picture our life as a cup. We must realize that we and others are pouring into our lives inputs of all kinds: friends, music, thoughts, actions, dreams, words, beliefs, and values.

We are never an empty cup.

Whatever is poured into the cup, will also be poured out. Negative in, negative out.

Change your inputs, change your outputs.

"That was my life," John said. "When I made the commitment to change the inputs into my life, I began to experience Success in school, discovered a new circle of affirming friends, began to grow in my spiritual walk, and let go of toxic, unfaithful relationships."

What are we pouring into our lives? What are we allowing others to pour into our lives? You cannot drive a car with an empty gas tank. In order to have the energy, courage, and strength to overcome hurts, lies, and challenges, we must take care of ourselves.

"Wait a minute, John," you might say to yourself. "This sounds like selfishness to me." Yes, it does, so let me share an illustration with you.

For those of us who have flown many times on commercial airlines, before every departure, we're treated to a riveting show of the safety features and procedures.

- "Ohhhhh, you lift UP on the seat belt buckle!"
- [Plane in nosedive] "So glad for these tiny floor lights!"
- "Thank goodness this seat cushion can float if we crash at 300 mph into the Atlantic Ocean!"

All kidding aside, there is one safety tip the flight crew covers every single time. "Should there be an unexpected loss of air pressure in the cabin, oxygen masks will drop from the ceiling." Do you remember what they say next?

"Place the mask on your face and tighten the straps to keep it in place. **If you're flying with children, ensure**

83

your oxygen is flowing before assisting them."
Doesn't that sound selfish?

Yes, it does. But if *you* don't have oxygen, you will not be able to help the little person that is completely dependent on you to have oxygen as well. And that is my point.

We are unable to care for others if we do not care for ourselves first.

Our tank of energy must be refueled somehow. Because we know ourselves the best, it's most important for us to identify what refuels us and regularly make it a priority to set aside time to be refreshed, re-energized, restored, and re-focused. This is why burnout happens in every walk of life.

In the early 2000's, an epidemic of meth abuse began to emerge in the Midwest. One of the most surprising segments of users: stay-at-home moms.

I say this all the time with admiration: my wife has the toughest job. Full-time moms, who do not have access to regular self-care, are just as vulnerable to alcohol, drug, and stimulant abuse as highly caffeinated stock brokers on Wall Street.

Without ample self-care, the ones tasked with caring for others will run out of energy, will burn out. This is true for men and women at home, in business leadership, in healthcare, in non-profits, in education, and in ministry. Self-care is one of the most loving habits we can have.

We will never be able to consistently add value to others without regularly adding value to ourselves.

So how do we know that we're giving ourselves healthy helpings of self-love, self-esteem, and self-care without being selfish? Great question! The next 4 keys will help us avoid the trap of focusing too much on ourselves.

Self-Awareness

Before I share the definition of awareness, let me quickly explain why I keep referring to Webster's dictionary.

In 2017, as I was researching and writing my first book, I resolved to look up every word of substance to learn the *actual, literal* meaning and origins of the word, not what I had thought for years, not what others' have said it is and not assuming what it could be. So many fresh revelations and surprising insights have come from just learning the full definition and origin of a word.

Thank you for your patience in bearing with me through these many definitions. I hope you will begin to explore the depth of meanings in weighty words to increase their impact in your life.

Awareness is defined as "knowledge or understanding that something is happening or exists." One aspect of this definition is current reality, what exists, and the other, what is happening, includes actions that determine future reality.

Both can change--what exists and what is happening. Here's what is so encouraging about awareness: when we change what's happening, we also end up changing what exists. Here's how this applies to us.

With the fresh foundation of What Winning is, and a positive, affirming understanding of Who We Are, we are freed to act on our dreams and goals—what's happening, resulting in a growing awareness of what we're able to achieve—what exists.

The opposite of Success is not failure. The opposite of Success is giving up, not trying at all.

Trying, failing, working, striving—these are all present tense, all ongoing efforts that contribute to our Success, to our Winning.

That's the encouraging aspect of self-awareness. In order to add value to others, we must balance a growing awareness of our potential with a healthy dose of honesty.

Great coaches do not sugar-coat, nor do they destroy. They inspire AND instruct. They coach AND critique. We must be willing to accept constructive criticism to grow personally, to achieve more, to accomplish our goals.

Do you know what the word criticism means? One of the definitions blew my mind! Here it is: "the art of evaluating works of art."

Wow! If you assumed, like I did just before reading this definition, that criticism is always negative, you and I were totally wrong.

Intent and content determine whether criticism is constructive or destructive. Both our perception and the motivation of the one giving it determine whether critical input builds us up or tears us down.

We must be humble enough to realize that there will always be ways to improve. Rather than seeking perfection—remember that progress is the goal, not perfection—we must embrace the fact that ***process improvement is a wonderful tool that encourages innovation, collaboration, and determination, resulting in celebration***, of one achievement after another. If we understand that there will always be something, some way, to do it better, criticism will become a powerful tool to maximize our potential.

When a sculptor is creating their work of art, using the chisel can be viewed as destructive. But is it truly? Yes, chunks of marble are being chipped away, so there is loss happening. But is it destructive?

Intent of the artist determines that. As the artist chisels away, a beautiful creation begins to emerge.

The same is true for constructive criticism. When the critic cares for us and wants our best, their input is designed to chip away the distractions that are holding us back from achieving our potential. They're not destroying us; they're liberating us.

But what if you do not have someone like this in your life right now? What if you're surrounded by people whose intent is not to build you up and help you reach your full potential? Are you stuck, without options? Not at all!

Self-Examination

On social media, I have seen an inspiring piece of graphic art that shows a well-muscled man, from the chest up, chiseling away at the excess from his waist down. The idea being that he is chipping away at the person he is now, to become the person he desires to be.

If you do not know a "sculptor"—a coach, a mentor, a positive person of influence—then *you* can pick up the chisel. But before you start hacking away, it's always best to have an idea of what you want to accomplish, what you want your sculpture to look like.

Two or three days a week, I wake up early in the morning, sluggishly change into workout clothes, and stumble out the door for a 30-minute workout. Not only am I starting off my day with exercise, I'm setting aside time to determine where I want to chisel my sculpture, where I can improve my life.

Self-examination is a powerful tool that is best applied unplugged from the busyness of life. No matter what time of day you choose, I highly recommend setting aside regular time for introspection, to identify areas of improvement, to reflect on progress made, and to help stay on track with goal-oriented priorities.

Life is all about change; nothing ever remains the same from day to day. Yes, experiences can be similar—where we live, where we work, the people in our lives—all these can be the same.

But unlike the premise of the movie *Groundhog Day* with Bill Murray, every day is a fresh opportunity to build on the Successful choices we made the day before. **Compound progress.** If we don't like the direction we're headed in or the choices we're making in life, we simply change them.

The only thing we can fully control in life is our choices—how we respond to life as it unfolds.

The greatest change we can experience in life is what we bring about ourselves.

Changes are going to happen no matter what. What we need to direct is the change that will impact us and others for our best. Here are some tips for effective, positive self-examination.

- Areas to improve are a good thing, so eagerly look for them

- Focus on how we can positively impact ourselves and others
- Fix the issue, not the blame
- Identify specific action steps, and take them!
- Inform trusted people of your plans for accountability
- Follow up with yourself to evaluate progress
- Keep track of your improvements; written form is best

Self-Motivation

In order to bring about lasting, positive change that adds value to others, we must diligently pursue it. While the encouragement of other people is a huge help, it's up to us to make this a priority.

Have you ever been around a self-motivated person? Of course, we have! What qualities stand out when you're around these people? Here are several aspects I admire:

- They take initiative
- They're creative
- They add value to others by their words and actions

- They focus on the solution rather than the problem
- They do not need extra incentives to do their very best
- They have an infectious, positive attitude
- They have a passion for learning

I love being around these people! And I'm committed to being one of them.

I know many people that are self-motivated. They have all types of personalities, life experiences, and career paths. The most exciting aspect of being self-motivated is that it's all up to us. No one and nothing in life can keep us from turning inspiration into action.

One more insight into self-motivation: it must never be based on how much or how little we have achieved. Why? If our motivation level is tied to our progress, our effort will go up and go down as the circumstances of our life ebb and flow. As a matter of fact, we must give even greater effort during the difficult times.

It's easy to be highly motivated when our life is on the mountain tops. It takes great inner strength to do our very best in the valleys.

Marathon runners call it "hitting the wall." In a 26-mile race, often at the 20th mile, the stored energy in their muscles is depleted, often forcing the athletes to slow down, walk, cramp, or even drop out of the race. At that point in the race, they've completed over 75% of the marathon.

Here are 7 techniques runners use to avoid "hitting the wall", and, as you read them, their application to our personal lives will intrigue you.

- ➢ Weekly long runs
- ➢ Hydration
- ➢ Eating right
- ➢ Adequate sleep
- ➢ Food during the race
- ➢ Pace
- ➢ Spectators

Preparation

Did you notice that of those 7 tips, more than half of them took place before the race even began? If you begin to look for sources of inspiration during the difficult times, it will be that much harder to remain motivated.

We must make self-motivation a daily priority, no matter the circumstances. The best time to cultivate healthy, strong self-motivation is during the smooth times in life. They'll prepare us for the times when we will need motivation the most.

Pace

The last two techniques had the most impact for me: pace and spectators (people). The running experts all advise setting a pace that can be maintained throughout the race. It can be tempting to start off too fast, matching our pace with the pack.

The same wisdom applies to life:

Don't set your pace of accomplishments or set goals based on others.

Don't be discouraged when it seems like others are finishing ahead of you or accomplishing more in life. That's not important.

Finishing the race is most important.

Beating *your* best time is important.

Staying healthy and running strong is important.

It's perfectly fine to use competition as a source of inspiration, but it must not be the only one. Just like we discussed in the first chapter, the healthiest comparison is our past self to our present self. We will be frustrated and disappointed, tempted to give up, if we focus too much on others.

People

There are many inspirational, heart-warming videos of other runners helping fellow athletes complete a marathon after they've "hit the wall" or suffered a minor injury. Even a crowd of strangers cheering has been proven to help marathoners run better.

It's not surprising that this critical element comes up time and again: the people in our lives. Spectators encourage us to do our best, and those running with us enable us to run well. We'll cover this priority thoroughly in the 6th chapter.

For self-motivation to be most effective, we must surround ourselves with others who are strongly self-motivated. Their confidence, Success, and encouragement will enable us to stay focused in order to finish well.

Selfless Service

During my basic training with the Army, we were taught an acronym-LDRSHIP. The letters stood for Loyalty, Duty, Respect, Selfless Service, Honor, Integrity, and Personal courage. I want to take a moment to reflect on the 4th item: Selfless Service.

One of the best ways to avoid being too much about ourselves is to devote time, energy, and money (when available) to give to others. According to the Cleveland Clinic and the National Institute of Aging, regular giving improves our health in the following 7 ways:

- Lower blood pressure
- Lower rates of heart disease
- Increased self-esteem
- Less depression
- Lower stress levels
- Longer life
- Greater happiness

We'll unfold the incredible power we all have access to through a life devoted to Giving in the last chapter. But, for now, read those 7 health benefits again. Who doesn't want a longer, happier, healthier life? I know I do!

That's the beauty of sincere, selfless service—it benefits us as well as the one who receives. If your life already includes intentional, regular giving, that's the only proof you need that you're not self-absorbed. No matter what the naysayers may falsely accuse, you truly care about others more than yourself.

One word of caution: just like Success, **do not** measure your "level" of giving against someone else's. This is pointless and potentially discouraging.

There have been times in our family's life when we were able to give in three ways: time, energy, and finances. Then there have been times where 1 of 3 ways of giving was all we could do—we were surviving as a family in the toughest times.

The best question to honestly ask yourself is not: "How much am I giving?" The right question is: "How am I giving?" and then "How can I give more without taking from the ones I love?"

Answer those two questions honestly, and you'll be encouraged (by how you give already) and inspired (to creatively find more ways to give).

Do It Now: Write down the ways you're giving to others in any way: financially, with your time, kind words, listening, encouraging. You'll discover you're giving more than you realize. Good for you! Keep doing it!

According to Giving USA, Americans gave over $400 billion to charity in 2017. And, remarkably, Charities Aid Foundation, a global giving research firm, found that more than 3 billion people gave to someone they didn't know in 2020, from a study that included 100+ countries. In the midst of a global pandemic!

People overwhelmingly give to others; the odds are that you do as well. Stop comparing how much you give, and start being grateful to be **able to give**, while exploring how to give more. The best tip I can share with you?

ASK. If you're looking for how to give to someone you know, ask them. "How can I help you?"—a very simple question, but so critically important. Here's why.

By asking open-ended questions, we can learn what is most important to the other person. By listening to them, we prove that we care about them. By giving intentionally and specifically, we can help meet their greatest need, which is often *not* financial.

And if their greatest need requires money, enlarge your vision to include others. Go Fund Me and other crowd-funding opportunities enable us to give very small amounts as a team that can add up to a significant sum. The effort to organize and coordinate a fundraiser on someone's behalf means far more than the limited funds you may be able to contribute yourself. Best of all, it enables others to give, sharing their care for you and your friend.

Self-less Service has more to do with looking and listening for opportunities to give, than about gallantry, duty, and laying our lives on the line for our country. I've had the privilege to do both, and I can tell you that far more people have the opportunity to change a life by how they give to others. The military does not have sole claim on Self-less Service; we all have access to this incredible privilege.

You are Special

I know, I know. Whenever we hear the phrase, "You're special", it does not always have a positive connotation to it! My good friends and I laugh at each other when we think about being called special by our loved ones. We were special, all right! Unique, anyways.

We can all agree that special typically means unique, different than something else, or standing out for one reason or another. Those definitions are all correct, but they're not the one I will use.

According to Webster's dictionary, here is the 5th definition for the word "special": "designed for a particular purpose or occasion."

Even more important than how we define what Winning is, we must employ the best definition for "special".

You were designed for a highly unique and very specific purpose. *Only you can fulfill that purpose.*

You're the only one qualified to rise to the occasion. There's only one John D. Hanson like me on the face of the earth and in all of human history. Did you catch that?

You're the only one like you.

Please do not just skip over this one sentence. Reflect on this truth for a moment with me.

Your fingerprints are literally one-in-64 billion! Just like snowflakes upon closer examination, people are highly unique. Snowflakes are all made with snow; people are all made with skin. But as you look much closer, our incredible uniqueness emerges.

Or how about trees? When I took a walk outdoors a little while ago, it struck me one morning that you can plant millions of apple trees, and yet not one will be exactly alike to another.

We're just like trees. We're all human, but our experiences in life, our shaping influences, our genetics, our choices—all add up to our life. And there's not a single life anywhere in this world or in history that has ever been, or ever will be, exactly the same.

If you truly realize the enormity of how uniquely special you are, the right question to ask is: "What am I here for?"

You were born at this time in history that you did not choose, by the parent or parents you did not choose, in the country you did not choose, with the genetics you did not choose so that *you could make a difference in the lives of others by what you choose.*

Powerful irony, and yet so beautiful and inspiring!

Ignore all the half-truths, lies, slander, and negativity that people have said to you and about you.

You're not their opinion of who you are. You are not what you have or have not accomplished.

You are who you were created to be and who you choose to be. THAT is all that matters.

Without a healthy, correct view of ourselves we will not be able to add value to others and have a fulfilling life.

Let me leave you with 7 aspects of Who you are that are unique only to you:

- Your non-negotiable core values---your character
- Your personality
- Your skills and abilities—what you've learned
- Your talents—what you were born with
- Your life experiences
- Your close relationships
- Your dreams

That very last item: your dreams. I have a powerful tool that can transform your dreams from a Wish to a Way. Let me share it with you now.

Winning Secrets: Who Are You?

My Menu

_____

_____

_____

_____

_____

_____

Chapter 3

When, Not If

"You are never too old to set a new goal

or to dream a new dream."

C.S. Lewis

I remember it as clearly today as I did in 2016. I was told by a well-meaning person, "John, you're too old to change your career. Just stay where you're working now and do your best there." I'm so glad I did not take that poor advice. Why?

Five career steps later, I continue to be entrusted with the best opportunities of my life.

Never listen to people who tell you that you're too old, too young, too experienced, too inexperienced, etc. The wonderful thing about dreams is that there is no expiration date. It's never too late (so long as we're alive!) to chase them down.

But how do we pursue our dreams? What if we're experiencing a valley in our lives, a tough time where we're hanging on just to survive? Or what if we're experiencing great Success in our current career or time in life that's not connected to a personal dream?

Great questions! I've been in both situations, and both can be challenging in their own way. It's easy to wish for better things when life is tough, and the way to get there does not seem possible or clear. And when life is going smoothly, why abandon the things that are providing a comfortable way of life?

Before I answer those important questions, let me share Kary's story with you.

Injury to Inspiration

Cutting. It's one of the categories of NSSI, or Non-Suicidal Self-Injury. A 2017 CDC study that researched emergency room visits for American youth uncovered a 20% annual increase in self-inflicted injuries. According to a study of college students by the Journal of American College Health, 15% of students shared that they had engaged in self-injury at least once. And these figures were gathered prior to COVID; they are most likely even higher now, with mental health issues at an all-time high for all ages. Until I began to look into this issue, I had no idea how many people were struggling with self-injury.

But what does this have to do with chasing our dreams? Everything. This is where Kary's story comes in.

When his mother and father both suffered severe health issues, Kary began to suffer from depression and anxiety over his deep pain and inability to control what was happening to his loved ones.

That's when he began to injure himself. It was one thing in his life that he could control. This harmful pattern continued for many years, even into marriage and a pastoral ministry.

When Kary finally mustered the courage to share his pain with one of his professors, rather than helping Kary heal, the man said he was not fit to counsel others and flunked him.

Immediately following that extremely painful experience, Kary injured himself again and suffered a breakdown. It was at that point, one of his lowest times in life, that he turned to God and counseling to heal himself. Rather than being consumed by pleasing others or looking like he had it all together, Kary realized that to help others, he had to heal first.

Sounds familiar, doesn't it? Self-care: one of the keys to Who We Are, found in the previous chapter. We must help ourselves first, in order to be able to help others who depend on us for their care.

Fast forward to today. Kary has had the privilege of inspiring, influencing, coaching, and mentoring over 250,000 authors, speakers, and coaches, has authored multiple best-selling books, and is the CEO and Founder of Igniting Souls Publishing Agency and host of the Blockchain Life podcast.

How did he grow from a life marked with Pain and Posing to a calling that Equips and Encourages others to transform their lives? By discovering his true identity, caring for himself, *then* pursuing his life calling. Just like Pat and John, those steps had to be in place first for Kary to Win, to Succeed.

Now let's add the next most important piece to Winning more—how Kary pursued his life calling.

One of the most important tools all the highly Successful people employ is goal setting. Kary calls it Unhackability: identifying, setting, and relentlessly pursuing his personal goals. I highly recommend getting all of Kary's books. For starters, get *Unhackable, Show Up*

Filled Up, and *Day Job to Dream Job.* All his titles will add significant value to your life and dream pursuits.

While it may seem like common sense to have goals in life, I was shocked to realize that I did not have them for so many years. And I'm not alone.

According to Brian Tracy, only 3% of Americans have written goals. And less than 1% review and rewrite their goals regularly. Global coaches I've interacted with share that they encounter a similar lack of written goals as well.

Yes, I had achievements I wanted to accomplish; most people do. When it comes to goals, most people do not. So what's the difference between what we want to achieve and goals?

Specific

The biggest difference between things we would like to achieve and goals is whether they're highly-specific or not. For example, you tell me, "John, I would like to buy a car."

"Great!" I reply. "Tell me about the car you would like to own."

"I'm not really sure what I want; there are so many options."

You have a desired achievement, a wish, but not a goal.

When I was 19, I knew **exactly** what car I wanted. A 2000 Pontiac Bonneville GT. Hunter green exterior, tan leather interior, V-6 engine, sport wheels package, with the deluxe audio package—CD/cassette/radio.

I just dated myself, I know! Some of you will be asking, "What is a cassette player?" At least I didn't say I wanted an 8-track player! [Google them for me ;) Let's just say we've come a *long* way!]

Here's my point. Saying you want a car and knowing what car you want is a HUGE difference. That's the difference between a wish and a goal.

One approach acts like it would be nice to have a car when you get around to it; the other uses highly specific choices that result in sitting behind the wheel of the car you want.

If your goals in life are not specific, the ebbs and flows of life, the circumstances, will shape your direction. You'll be like a raft rather than a canoe. Don't let the current take you where it wants you to go. You choose where you want to go, and paddle like crazy until you arrive. Let me share an example from my life.

When I returned from Iraq in 2011 while serving with the Ohio Army National Guard, the hunt for a civilian job began. It took 6 months to secure a great-paying job with Chase as a senior loan processor. I was hired during the refinance boom in 2012, so business was more than our team could handle. Despite the extremely high caseload, my productivity was strong, and my customer satisfaction ratings were always at the top of my team. Unlimited overtime resulted in some very cool paychecks, too!

But, like any boom, the refinance surge did not last. At the beginning of 2013, the demand for refinances began to slow. Teams were consolidated under fewer managers as caseloads resumed to normal levels. I had confidence that my performance metrics would keep me in the mortgage processing group. I was wrong.

In the fall of 2013, hundreds of processors were told they had 120 days to find a new position within Chase—our positions were being terminated. The sad irony of it all was that the colleague sitting right next to me, with less seniority, lower performance metrics, and who consistently needed my help to complete daily tasks, that person was kept on and I was laid off.

How did I get blindsided? How did I miss those massive changes that were coming? Why did I assume that I would be kept on the team?

I was a raft, not a canoe. I had no specific career goals. As a result, I was not making decisive career moves to advance within Chase.

I learned a huge lesson:

Being productive is not the same as pursuing our dreams.

Being productive, accomplishing key tasks, being recognized for superior work, and adding value to our team—these are neutral activities. They can be tied to chasing our dreams or tied to nothing at all. That's why having specific goals is critically important. Doing a great job makes us great team members; it does not mean that we are Winning greatly.

Set them, See them

So how do we set our goals? Here are some tips on how to set specific goals that are more effective---helping to make our goals more likely to be achieved.

As simple as this seems, write them down. That's correct—physically write them down on a piece of paper. A University of Kansas study found that written goals are achieved 30% more often than goals only in our minds. 30%--that's a big difference! But why is writing them down so important?

The study revealed that writing connects our conscious mind with our subconscious. It translates thoughts into desire, and our subconscious begins to work on achieving what we wrote. Our mind is a supercomputer, always working in the background. While we're focusing on the tasks at hand, it's constantly processing our desires and goals. Even while we're sleeping, our mind is at work. That's why we often dream about people or events that prompt strong emotions, often tied to relationships or desires that are very important to us. Our subconscious mind weaves those key experiences into our dreams.

Writing down our goals makes a physical record. This adds importance to our goals, as well as something we can see with our eyes. Everything we see with our eyes is processed by our subconscious mind.

So, post your specific, written goals where you can see them throughout the day—on your computer, on your desk, in the car, in your room.

Along with the written goal, post a picture of what you will own or an experience you will have when you achieve your goal. Pictures and words together are even more powerful for our subconscious mind—the engine for our motivation, inspiration, and determination.

Winning Secret #5: Be what you see!

Cameron graduated almost dead last in his high school class with a 1.05 GPA and got his first job washing dishes in a restaurant for $2.65 an hour. On his first try to enter culinary school, he was turned away because his grades were too low.

Today, Cameron Mitchell owns over 50 restaurants across the U.S., valued at $300 million. What was one priority to which he credits his Success? Written goals. To this day, Mr. Mitchell keeps a legal pad with him at all times in order to keep his written, specific goals in front of him.

Written goals work!

Do It Now: Write down your highly specific goals, with a picture of the item/experience, if you'd like, and post them throughout your home, vehicle, and workplace.

Stamp it!

This small step is very important—put a date stamp on your specific, written goals. The immediate response to this idea is often, "But, John, what if I set a date and don't achieve my goal?"

My question in response would be, "What if you don't set a date, and don't achieve your goal?"

The reluctance to set a date springs from a natural concern that we will be disappointed if we don't achieve our goal by the time we set for ourselves. But that is why we *must* set a date.

We cannot use an infinite timeline to achieve our dreams. Someday becomes Never.

I can guarantee that you'll be closer to achieving your goal if you put a date to it. Here's why.

CTA—Call To Action. In the advertising/marketing world, Call To Action is the critically important tool used to convert a prospect to a client. It's the bottom-line difference between a lead and a conversion (converting a lead to a customer, resulting in a sale). Some would argue, correctly, that a Call To Action is the most important part of a website or ad campaign. Why?

Without the Call To Action, you're *hoping* the customer chooses your product or service (the raft). With a highly specific, well-crafted Call To Action, you are persuading the interested party to select you (the canoe). Is Amazon wishing people will buy or influencing them to buy? Are we wishing our goals will happen or taking steps to make them happen?

General George S. Patton was a flamboyant, highly Successful tank commander in World War II. His ability to inspire his officers and soldiers to achieve seemingly impossible tasks was legendary. One of his quotes resonated strongly with me in regard to time-stamping our goals: "Never tell people how to do things. Tell them what to do, and they will surprise you with their ingenuity."

By setting a date, we're telling ourselves *what* needs to be accomplished, requiring us to figure out *how* to achieve it. With a date "set in stone", we now must come up with a plan on how we will achieve it. It's a personal Call To Action.

Put a date stamp on your goals today and watch how ingenious you become to achieve them by that date.

Tony Robbins said, "If you talk about it, it's a dream; if you envision it, it's a possibility, but if you schedule it, it's real." It's not Magical, but it surely is Motivating!

Stunning and Stretching

A book I highly recommend for your reading list is *Built to Last* by Jim Collins. This best-selling book reveals key principles that enable companies to succeed for generations.

One principle in the book is cited widely by renowned authors, speakers, and advisors—BHAG's. Big Hairy Audacious Goals. If your goals do not seem over-the-top or audacious to you ("I shouldn't even be saying this", for example), then they're not bold enough.

In order for creativity, innovation, and collaboration to feel necessary, the end goal must be daunting, like climbing Mt. Everest. Every-day, boring goals that are easily achieved do not inspire, like walking in the park. Yes, if our goals seem "like a walk in the park" versus "climbing Mt. Everest", they're not bold enough! Pun intended.

If our highly specific, time-stamped, written goals do not light a fire under us, then our motivation to take decisive action steps will "run out of steam." That saying comes from the days of the steam locomotive. In order for the engine to have power, the fire hopper had to be constantly fed with wood or coal. No fire, no steam. No steam, no power. No power, no progress. The same is true for us: No specific BHAG's, no motivation. No Motivation, no progress.

Goals are great, but without a burning desire to achieve them, without a compelling motivation, they will not be reached. Or it will take far too long to reach them.

For many years, I wished I could write a book that would add value to others. Once I knew what I was going to write about, then I put the time, effort, research, and steps in place to achieve it. The result? I achieved something remarkable, according to Joseph Epstein. A renowned writer, Epstein stated that up to 81% of Americans (over 200 million people) feel that they have a book in them but have yet to write it. That's a lot of people with unfulfilled dreams! Imagine how many people in the world think the same way.

By setting goals, I was blessed to learn so much and complete a quality resource that is a growing encouragement to more and more people who value a world-class customer experience. It would not have happened without highly specific goals, without keeping my end goal in front of me daily, without putting a date to when I was going to publish the book, and without motivating myself to achieve a daunting task.

How about you? What dreams do you have? Do they seem so far-fetched that you have given up trying to reach them? Have the challenges of life slowed you down or discouraged you from chasing your dreams? One thing I can tell you: it's never too late to start.

Start today by setting bold, audacious goals that seem shocking to you. Take what you would like to do and multiply its impact.

Along with writing a book, which I did, my audacious goal now is to impact 1 million people by the year 2029. Bold, isn't it? As time goes on, I expect that this will no longer seem like a nearly impossible feat, but quite doable. Guess what will happen then?

I will set a new and daring goal that will stretch me and stun others. If our dream doesn't stretch us, we won't grow. If our dream isn't stunning, it won't shock us into action. Make your big, bold dreams Stretching and Stunning!

Sequential

I promise you, this next section has nothing to do with math! So what do I mean by Sequential?

Remember in the first chapter, we talked about Compound Progress—Successes and failures that build on one another to reach the ultimate goal? We should set goals with this in mind. Yes, we need to establish the ultimate dream for motivation and inspiration.

Just as important, we also need to identify the goals along the way to reaching that ultimate goal. Setting and achieving sequential goals keeps us encouraged, motivated, and on track. If we only focused on the ultimate goal, which often takes years to accomplish, we would easily become distracted or discouraged.

Winning the championship in any sport requires far, far more sequential goals than the ultimate goal. Great coaches can keep their team focused on achieving their best in every practice, every video session, every one-on-one coaching, and every game.

That's why at almost every press conference, the great coaches will never say that their goal is to Win the national or world championship. Of course, that's what they want to achieve, or they would be coaching for nothing!

So why do they always downplay the importance of Winning the championship trophy? Because the sequential goals along the way are more important. It's the same way for us.

In order to aggressively pursue our dreams, we must set and chase after the smaller, progressive goals that will get us there. In the case of writing a book, if I only focused on my published work of 160 pages, full-color cover, and website, I would've never completed that project. I had to break it down, setting aside time to create outlines, brainstorm, and research in order to put words on paper. Those small, daily priorities, over time, added up to a finished work, the book "*WOW Your Customers! 7 Ways to World-Class Service.*"

Our lives are far more complex, with relationships and responsibilities requiring our attention and best effort.

This is another reason why smaller, sequential goals are so important. They are doable.

The Big, Hairy Audacious Goals (BHAG's) are long-term; they will take a long time and many steps to get there. If my BHAG was to own a Pontiac Bonneville, then I would set sequential goals to get there. So many dollars saved from so many paychecks would add up to enough to buy the car, over time.

"But how do I stay motivated if the end goal is more exciting than the sequential goals along the way?" Great question! The answer goes back to Be What You See. We need to be able to see the progress we're making. But how do you do that with a major goal or purchase?

In the case of the car, I would print or draw (not me, my drawing is horrible!) a black-and-white poster of the car I want. As I earn money, I would color in the paper car with hunter green (one of my favorite colors) in the amount that represents the share of the car I could buy with the money I had just earned.

For example, if the car costs $25,000, and one of the two wheels visible in the picture is a tenth of the entire white space, every $500 saved would color 1/5 of a wheel. As the hunter green grows and covers more & more of the picture, my mind sees that I'm getting closer and closer to my ultimate goal. Then something very cool happens.

My mind begins to tell me, "John, if you set aside a little bit more each paycheck, or spend a little less this month, you could have the Bonneville even sooner!" That's the exciting aspect of setting and achieving sequential goals. As our Compound Progress grows, we begin to realize how our diligent effort, day in & day out, is getting us closer to our big dream. And that motivates us to go after the end goal even harder!

Share it!

If you thought that sequential goal setting was an awesome concept, check this next one out! All the ideas we've discussed so far are individual tools. This next concept will result in mind-blowing results, I promise you! So here it is—share your BHAG with others. If this seems underwhelming, let me explain a little more.

The power of this goal-achieving principle came to life in May of 2019. I had reached a point in writing this book that the introduction and first chapter were well-established. But I had hit a wall for the content of the remaining 6 chapters. The outlines and key principles of each chapter were identified, but no words were flowing when I sat down to write. I'm committed to never manufacturing content—writing words for the sake of simply filling pages. My content needs to be authentic, moving, and encouraging. Here's where the power of sharing my dreams kicked in.

It hit me—everyone knows the Success stories of famous icons, that they did not achieve fame and influence overnight. So many people, including myself, know that these life experiences are true, but we don't feel that they're relatable. I'm not an inventor like Thomas Edison, or an athlete like Michael Jordan, or an entertainment mogul like Oprah. Billions and billions of people will never be known around the world for who they are & what they do. I certainly fit into that category.

"That's kind of a downer, John. How the heck is this supposed to inspire me to Win more?"

I realized that in order for my book on Winning to have impact for millions of people, they must be able to relate to it. So I determined to contact highly-Successful people in my home state of Ohio to learn about their stories and principles of Success.

Not only did I leave every single interview impressed and inspired, but I **knew**, beyond the shadow of a doubt, that the power of sharing their life lessons with my readers would prove to be far more powerful than reminding them of the famous Success stories of famous people we all know.

Once I realized how I was going to infuse authentic, invaluable content into my book, I began to excitedly share this concept with everyone who would listen. I sent multiple requests through social media to interview influential, Successful people in various industries. I attended a local workshop comprised of aspiring authors to encourage and to be encouraged.

"So you got an idea for content for your book? *That's* the "power" of sharing your ideas with others, John? Not impressed." Nope; that's just the beginning. Listen to the rest of the story.

In the space of 60 days, I connected with over 3,500 people on Facebook, received the endorsement of a renowned speaker & author, added an incredible business mentor, was invited to a nationally distributed podcast, connected with an international speaker & corporate trainer, and met with a social media influencer with over 3 million downloads. Best of all, my BHAG exploded from publishing my 2nd book with world-wide impact to impacting 1 million people by the year 2029. What brought about all these incredible, life-changing events?

Sharing my dream with others. But not just anyone.

We'll get into greater detail on this in the 6th chapter, so I will simply say:

Share your BHAG with people who also have BHAG's.

It's that simple, but that powerful. Only people who have audacious goals will encourage you to chase after your stunning & stretching achievements.

<u>Do It Now</u>: Identify 3 or 4 people you trust to share your goals with every week. Ask if they would be willing to receive a weekly email tracking your progress towards your BHAG's. They do not need to follow up with you, unless they choose to do so. Sending them a weekly summary is the accountability you need to keep pursuing your dreams. Try it; it works!

That's 6 keys to Winning more by setting written, specific, time-stamped, stunning & stretching, sequential goals and sharing them with others. So what's the 7th key to goal setting? I'm glad you asked!

Satisfied

The last key has nothing to do with setting or pursuing our goals. What? That doesn't make sense! Hang in there with me, and I promise it will all come together in this last principle.

Winning—we have a fresh, inspiring definition for what it is. In relation to setting & pursuing our goals, Winning has nothing to do with where we've been or where we are right now. That's all been accomplished. Setting goals for something that has already been achieved is pointless. However, one critical aspect of our humanity is in danger if we neglect this last principle—satisfaction.

Guess where we're going? That's right—back to the dictionary! Webster's defines satisfaction as: "the quality or state of being satisfied: contentment" and "a source or means of enjoyment: gratification." Two powerful truths, life-changing truths, need to be unpacked here.

Did you notice that satisfaction is on-going? *"**Being** satisfied."* We must work to be content. Let me start with what is **not** being content.

Contentment is **not** settling, and it is **not** getting comfortable. Contentment is a state of mind that appreciates what we have achieved, who we're connected with, and where we have arrived in life, so far. It's enjoying the journey on the way to our ultimate destination.

If we're too busy, too tired, or too stressed to recognize the incredible life experiences and relationships we have, then we're too busy, working too hard, or discontent. So what's the difference between being content and settling for a comfortable, easy life?

While they may look the same, it only requires a few key questions, answered honestly, to reveal which state we're in:

- Are we happy?
- Are we surrounded by people who love and value us?
- Are we compassionate and kind to others?
- Are we encouraged by the challenges we've overcome?
- Are we excited about the lessons we've learned?
- Are we amazed by the value we've added to others?
- Are we looking forward to the journey still to come?

If we're not happy with what we've achieved in life, then we will never be satisfied, never content.

It's a dangerous mindset to be infatuated with how much farther ahead we **should be**, without realizing how much farther ahead we **are**.

One source of happiness should come from the self-awareness that we've accomplished a great deal in life, as well as what we already possess.

Remember in the first chapter we talked about the need to compare our present selves to our past selves, in order to gain a clear understanding of our progress, our Success.

What have you achieved? Make a list. That's right. Make a list of everything you've achieved. With all that you've read in these three chapters, the list should be extensive! Take into account major life milestones like key relationships, career, education, and childhood dreams you've achieved.

Do It Now: Make a list of all the achievements you've accomplished in your life. Go all the way back to being a kid—what did you achieve that was beyond normal for you? Be truthful and be generous. DON'T COMPARE YOURSELF TO OTHERS!

After you've created that list, now reflect on what you have: possessions, life experiences, friendships, close relationships, talents, skills & abilities, health, etc. When I reflected on what we're blessed with, it brought a familiar verse from the Bible to mind: "Food, clothing and shelter--- with these we should be content."

Our lives are filled with abundance, especially when we look at them through a grateful, content point of view.

Do It Now: Make a list of all the blessings in your life, all the things, experiences, and people you have. My hope is that your list ends up being much larger than you anticipated. Look how much you have to be grateful for!

One last word of caution: as you create these lists, please do not allow comparison to steal your joy and gratitude. My good friend, Renee Vidor, has written a powerful book entitled, *"Measuring Up: How to WIN in a World of Comparison."* I highly recommend that you add this book to your reading list. Comparison can be a deadly poison to gratefulness and contentment when we compare ourselves to others.

Distract, Diminish, Dull

Don't allow the blessings of your highly Successful life to be dulled by your perception of others' Success. Distance yourselves from those who boast or self-promote to feel better about themselves. Focus on **your** goals, **your** dreams, **your** blessings, **your** journey.

Being content does not mean stopping on the path of life and sitting on a park bench for the rest of your life. It's realizing that the journey is more important than the destination, being grateful for the invaluable, memorable experiences along the way.

Don't worry about how long this journey seems to be taking. Enjoy, learn, connect, and reflect as you pursue your dreams.

Grateful, content people are always a blessing to others, because they're never focused on themselves more than those around them. Isn't that one of the best definitions for Winning? Adding value to those around you will **always** result in a highly Successful life.

Why would a man take scalding-hot baths for 15 minutes over and over again, on purpose!, until he almost passed out? Find out what that remarkable discipline has to do with Winning, in the next chapter!

Winning Secrets: When, Not If

My Menu

_____

_____

_____

_____

_____

_____

_____

Chapter 4

Will to Win

"Never, never, never give up!"

Winston Churchill

Goal Getting

Why on earth would a person immerse themselves in scalding-hot Epsom salt baths for 25-minute periods with only their face out of the water?!

Sounds like torture, doesn't it? If you asked Ken Wentworth, a.k.a. Mr. Biz, he would tell you that it was one of the most physically rigorous times in his life, even more demanding than training.

Training? Training for what?

To set the world record for power lifting in his weight class. The lower the weight at weigh-in the day before the event, the greater the advantage a lifter has when they're fully recovered, rehydrated, and replenished the day of the event. But his incredible weight-shedding process didn't start with the scalding hot baths.

12 weeks out from the event, he worked his way up to drinking 3 GALLONS of water, PER DAY. You read that right—384 ounces of water every.single.day. For 3 months. Can you imagine how many trips to the bathroom that would take?!

Now comes the weight cutting day. This is where it gets intense. 4 ½ hours before weigh-in, Ken had to lose 17 pounds. Yes, you read that right—17 pounds in less than 5 hours!

After soaking for 25 minutes, it took him 5 minutes just to get out of the tub without passing out. 30 minutes of rest on the bed, weight check, then back in the tub for another 25 minutes.

Normally, Ken would repeat this process 2-3 times and be good to go. But this time, that didn't do the trick. 6 baths in, and still not down to the required 165 pounds.

But Ken was going for a new world record, and he was not going to quit now.

One bath after another, until Mr. Biz reached the 165-pound goal. He was so exhausted at that point, that his 2 training partners literally carried him to the weigh in.

If you're like me, you might be asking yourself, "Who on earth would want to do all that?!"

A person who doesn't just set goals for motivation, but gets them, too. The same person who said he would bench press 500 pounds right after lifting 275 pounds. That guy.

The first time Ken and I had coffee, we talked for 4 hours. Time flew for me. I gained so much from Ken's Can-Do attitude, his determination & dedication, and record-setting achievements.

I highly recommend getting a copy of Mr. Biz' book, Don't Fake The Funk, where he lays out the process he used to achieve multiple world records---the same processes you can use to achieve your own audacious goals.

While his achievements in the business world and in athletics were impressive, what was most striking for me was that a person would never guess that Mr. Biz was a world record holder in powerlifting. He just doesn't fit the stereotypical image of a person who could repeatedly set power lifting records. But he did have one game changing attribute to achieve those massive goals.

Grit

One of my must-read recommendations is a book by Angela Duckworth entitled just that: *Grit*.

In her study of West Point cadets, Angela determined the #1 factor most likely to result in their graduation as officers in the U.S. Army. But let's start with what the most important factor **wasn't**. It was not:

Athleticism

Intelligence or IQ

Upbringing

Leadership skills

It was Grit. Simply---never giving up. It was Vince Lombardi who said, "The difference between a Successful person and others is not a lack of strength, not a lack of knowledge, but rather a lack of will." Well said.

But there's more to Grit than doggedly staying the course; there are 2 more aspects. As always, it starts with us—Inside Out---connecting two key drivers of long-term Success: Passion & Purpose.

Using an automobile as our analogy, Passion is the fuel, and our Purpose is the engine. There's much debate about which is more important. But let's not waste your time debating this. Let's embrace the fact that both are interdependent. Without the other, the fuel or the engine are full of potential that can never be realized without combining the two. And so it is for our Passions and our Purpose.

Once we become fully aware of what our deepest Passions and greatest Purpose(s) is/are, then we can turn our attention to the 2nd aspect—Outside In. We limit our impact, influence, and inspiration if our Grit never becomes contagious.

John Maxwell wisely pointed out that Winning alone is an empty achievement: "If you're at the top of a mountain alone, you're not a leader; you're a hiker." He also famously observed that leadership is influence. There are few attributes more conducive to team Success than contagious Grit.

If you've got Grit like that, pass it on to others just as hungry as you, looking for kindred spirits with Can Do attitudes. In the right culture, your team will become unstoppable with infectious Grit.

Gumption

I love that word! My wife says I'm an old soul, that I regularly use words that are from several generations ago. Gumption is one of those words. But it has such rich meanings, it would be selfish of me to keep it from you! Let me introduce this word to you through a story.

When I was a little boy, I distinctly remember a children's book entitled, The Little Engine That Could. A little red engine breaks down on its way to deliver food and toys to the children on the other side of a big mountain. The clown riding on the train flags down one engine after another: the shiny yellow passenger train, the big black freight train, and the rusty old locomotive. All of them decline to help.

Then a little blue engine, that switches train cars in the yard, happens by. Willing to help but unsure due to her size, she agrees to try. As she strains to pull the cars up and over the big mountain, she repeats to herself the mantra, "I think I can, I think I can, I think I can."

That's gumption—taking on a task that appears too big to handle and pulling it off with determination. The big freight train and the shiny yellow passenger train were more than capable but didn't want to be bothered. The old rusty engine didn't have the heart to take on the task. But the little blue engine wanted to help and gave it her all. And the children on the other side of the mountain enjoyed their much-needed food and beloved toys.

Don't be intimidated by the big freight trains in life. These people come off as powerful, busy, and productive. In reality, they're often posing, using social media or self-promotion to project an illusion, a false reality only meant to serve themselves.

Don't be disheartened by those who have given up, who no longer try to achieve their potential.

Be the Little Engine That Could, have gumption, say to yourself, "I can" so that you can proudly say, "I did."

The Gift of Failure

Think about it. If achieving massive goals was easy, everyone would experience massive Success. If everyone was experiencing massive Success, how special would those achievements be?

The fact that massive goals require incredible Will to Win is what makes their achievement special, memorable, extra-ordinary. And that's why we should always view What Didn't Work, i.e., Failure, as a gift.

"Are you crazy, John?!" Wouldn't be the first time others may have thought that about me! Hear me out.

If something isn't going to work, when would you rather find out? Sooner or later? One month later or 1 year down the road?

We must shift our mindset on Failure. After giving it our all, to see it as a competitive advantage. The faster a bad idea fails, the sooner we can adjust and go after it again. Let me share a perfect example with you.

You've more than likely used at least one Dyson product in your lifetime, whether it be hand dryers, hair dryers, fans, or vacuum cleaners. But do you know how many years and attempts it took James Dyson to Successfully invent his remarkable vacuum cleaner?

5 years and 5,127 attempts.

Read that line one more time.....slowly.

5 YEARS.

Over 5,000 ATTEMPTS.

Now, imagine yourself in THAT process. Why on earth would Mr. Dyson choose to fail over and over and over again?

Because he KNEW he had a good idea, just like Thomas Edison and the light bulb. Every failure---every time his prototype did not work---he grew one attempt closer to the time when it would work. Failure did not stop James Dyson, Thomas Edison, That Little Engine That Could, and many other highly Successful people.

And it shouldn't stop you.

Yes, you must KNOW, without a doubt, that you're on the right track. When you do, don't let anything keep you from pursuing your dreams.

When we're going through difficult times, and we're frustrated, disappointed that we're not even meeting our own goals and expectations for ourselves or our loved ones, that's actually a very good sign. It doesn't feel good, but it reveals that we're not content with settling for less or settling for nothing at all. We believe that things can be better, and we want to get there.

It's far better to be frustrated that we're not where we want to be, than to be OK with not even knowing where we're going or what we're doing or why we're doing it. That's

140

the difference between an intentional life, where we're always striving for more, and a purposeless life, where we exist rather than Excel.

Embrace Failure as a resource, as a continuous improvement tool, that will help you achieve your ultimate goal. Do you think the uber-Successful businesses like Chick-fil-a figured out their polished system in a day or two? That WOULD be crazy talk!

Failure is the flip side of the coin of Winning. We'll have Failures and Successes on the path to Winning at life. In order to possess the coin of Winning, we must be willing to work through the Failures on one side so that we can celebrate the Wins on the other.

Get back up

You've likely read this quote on social media countless times: "Fall down 7 times, stand up 8." It's an ancient Japanese proverb with timeless impact. This mindset has served me well throughout my life: basic training in the military; learning a new skill or task; riding a bicycle; exploring magic as a kid; playing football with the neighbors; watching our children in martial arts;

remembering our little ones taking their first steps while learning to walk.

No one mocks a baby for falling time and time again while their body figures out motor skills, balance, and forward motion. So why are we and others so hard on ourselves when we get older?

Because we lose sight of what's most important in any learning curve: getting back up.

The steps with the greatest impact often begin with the simplest action.

Thoughts, emotions, intentions, plans, and strategies can all be good things. But taking decisive action, especially when we may not feel like it, that's where the "secret" to long-term Success begins. Fall down, get right back up.

Kieran Behan

That name probably doesn't ring a bell for you. That's okay—it didn't for me either. I was doing a Google search for an inspiring story to best illustrate this point of getting up, no matter how many times we fall down. Kieran's story fit the bill perfectly.

Kieran was the first male gymnast to represent Ireland in the Olympics, and he did it twice. But that's not the most remarkable part of his story. We start with his childhood for that!

At 10 years old, Kieran was diagnosed with cancer in his thigh, requiring major surgery, accompanied by a one-year recovery from sitting in a wheelchair and a prognosis from the doctors that he might never walk again. But he did.

Fall down, get back up again.

15 months after a full recovery, Kieran suffered a severe fall during practice that resulted in a major head injury. This caused inner ear damage, affecting his balance. Once again, confined to a wheelchair, he had to learn how to sit and even move his head. It took 3 years to mend from that injury, with the doctors, once again, warning that he might never walk again. He fully recovered.

Fall down, get back up again.

In 2010, before competing in the European Championships, Kieran underwent ACL surgery, and fully recovered, returning to gymnastics and Winning several events.

Fall down, get back up again.

In 2012, Kieran qualified for the Olympics, but the Irish Olympic Committee refused to fund him. So he raised his own funding through bake sales and fund drives. He Successfully entered the 2012 Olympics as the first Irish gymnast.

Fall down, get back up again.

In 2015, he qualified for the European Olympics, the first Irish gymnast to do so, and in 2016, qualified for the Olympics in Rio. This time, he did NOT need to raise his own funding!

Following the Rio Olympics, Kieran underwent full knee replacement surgery and retired from competing, shifting his focus to coaching gymnastics. He is currently the Head Junior National Coach of Austria.

Fall down, get back up again.

Kieran overcame tremendous obstacles, again and again. He earned recognition and victories by simply getting back up again. And so can you.

Get to work

Not only is our definition of Winning incorrect, but how it's supposed to feel is wrong as well. Winning, in actuality, feels like hard work, devoted diligence, never giving up. That's Winning.

Winning is the process, the unwavering commitment, that results in overcoming. Winning is not when we reach the top of the mountain; Winning is the climb to get there.

Winning Secret #6: The Will to Win

I recently realized that the very word "Winning" is in the present tense, not a past tense. Those who are Win**ning** at life are *on their way* to the mountain tops of Success where they can say they have Won.

No one has ever achieved anything great instantly.

How completely ridiculous would it be to expect Warren Buffet to become a billionaire as soon as he invested his first dollar, or Michael Jordan to Win an NBA Finals as soon as he picked up a basketball, or Michael Phelps to swim to an Olympic gold the first time he swam a lap, or Serena Williams a Grand Slam tennis championship when she picked up a racket?

I'm overstating my case to make a very strong point: Winning is not the trophy. Winning is the day-in, day-out work to be ready to earn the trophy. You notice I did not say, grueling work to get the trophy. Winning is positioning ourselves in the best way to achieve our ultimate goal when the opportunity presents itself.

Simply put, it's impossible to work if we're not ready to work. And that's our last point on Grit.

Get ready

The word "Opportunity"—that's a book in and of itself! I took a trip to the dictionary, as I often do, to learn about its origin.

Turns out, it comes from the old sailing days, having to do with the whole process of getting from one "port" to another---op"port"unity.

Without giving away the punch line of my future book, let me quickly share the 7 points of how we can seize Opportunity.

1. Know where you want to go—ultimate destination
2. Gather the right people to make the trip—can't sail the big ship alone

3. Train through everyday routines to perfect teamwork skills

4. Prepare beyond what's needed; life happens!

5. Set the sails to catch the wind. Not ready for wind? Not ready to sail

6. Constant steering to keep the ship on course

7. Consult navigation tools to stay on course

One more point: when you arrive, celebrate with those who made it possible!

Opportunity isn't about luck. Highly Successful people, people who are constantly Winning at life, prepare for the next big break, confident it will come.

"There are no secrets to Success. It is the result of preparation, hard work and learning from failure." Colin Powell

Oh, by the way, Mr. Biz set a new world record in the 165-pound weight class for powerlifting. Yes, definitely yes--our Will to Win matters. It makes a world of difference for us and those who join us on our journeys to Success.

Speaking of those who join us, that's what the very next chapter is about.

Winning Secrets: Will to Win

My Menu

_____

_____

_____

_____

_____

_____

Chapter 5

Why and Who For

"People don't buy what you do; they buy why you do it."

Simon Sinek, author, *Start With Why*

If you've had the privilege of encountering Simon Sinek's material on *Start with Why*, whether by video or in print, then you probably remember the time and the place. Why?

Because of the "light bulb" moment that happens when leaders and learners like you and me discover the deepest motivator for ourselves and our team members--- our Why.

Our Deepest Why

Another excellent book I completed is called *The Lean Startup* by Eric Reis. One of the main points in the book begins with sharing the Lean Manufacturing Process that Toyota originated years ago, that has become the standard for industrial continuous improvement.

A key aspect of the Lean Process is unearthing root causes. Mr. Reis explained that the best way to discover the real cause of the problem was to ask the question "Why?" 5 times.

Not only does this work well in manufacturing, I've used this process during workshops, trainings, and in my personal life, to uncover the deepest motivators. The light bulb moments we've experienced have been eye opening and enlightening.

Take a moment now. Ask yourself "Why?" 5 times. For your personal & professional life, ask yourself "Why?", why are you pursuing these goals, for each. Do it 5 times. What you'll find is your deepest Why.

Do It Now: Write down your Top 3 Motivators. For each one, ask yourself 5 times, "Why is that important to me?" You'll be fascinated to discover what your deepest Motivators are!

The first time I completed this exercise, I realized that the B.H.A.G. (Big Hairy Audacious Goals, as Jim Collins calls them) that I set for myself were NOT my strongest motivators. Mine were connected to my family and my personal faith.

Seriously, take a pause from reading this book (I know it's sooo hard to put it down 😊), and complete this exercise for 3 things: your personal life, your professional life, and your biggest goal/dream.

While my big goals and dreams do motivate me, they're not the strongest drivers for relentlessly chasing my dreams. If getting from point A to point B is the goal, then being chased by a ravenous grizzly bear is our deepest Why. Extreme example, I know. But when the daily grind hits us squarely in the face, we need one of our strongest drivers to kick in, to keep us motivated, to keep us going.

Find your Deepest Why, and you'll unlock a Winning Secret that the highly Successful people use every day.

And if you want to influence, lead, or help others, ask them: "Would you mind if I asked you a personal question?" When they say, "Yes," ask them what their Why is, 5 times. You'll help them discover what deeply drives them to Win at life.

Our Strongest Why—Winning Secret #7

There's no greater motivator on the face of the earth than our loved ones. "Wait a minute, John! What about our deepest motivator?"

My deepest Why, I discovered, is not my strongest Why. Using the grizzly bear analogy again, imagine one of your little ones was being chased by that bear. Your safety and wellbeing would be of no consideration in a situation like that. You would do everything in your power to rescue your child.

Do you remember when you were younger and single—no children, no partner? Your deepest Why was probably your strongest motivator. But when we begin providing for others, loving others, those relationships become our strongest Why.

Think of the hard-working men and women you admire that work diligently throughout the week, sometimes at jobs they don't like, to provide for their families. Single moms juggling work, school, daycare, and life for their kids. People who labored in factories or skilled trades for 20 or 30 years, setting aside for their kids, grandkids, and retirement.

It's what keeps me going every day. I've realized that since being married and having children, I've called off work far fewer times. Much of the credit for that goes to my wife, who took better care of me than I did of myself! I tell others, "The Army made me strong, but my wife made me healthy!" She's a huge reason why I enjoy going to work, adding value to others, and chasing my career goals. I want to support her goals and dreams. My work is one way I do that.

Don't sell yourself short. Heroism is not reserved for Hollywood, the military, healthcare providers, first responders, or educators. Heroism is defined as the pursuit of two ideals: a higher purpose and excellence. If you do your best work every time and are doing it for others, you ARE a Hero. You ARE Winning at life.

I can't think of anything more Heroic than coming through day after day for the ones depending on you. If you don't come through, they have no one else to turn to. That's Heroic; that's Winning at life. That's your Heroic Why. We'll explore this in greater depth a little later in this chapter.

Martin CSI

Wait a minute?! Did the *CSI* franchise come out with **another** series?! Thank heavens, no! (I mean, unless you were eagerly awaiting *CSI Boise* ☺)

Martin CSI (Martin Control Systems, Inc.) is a privately owned industrial automation integration firm located in the Columbus, Ohio metro area. Companies like Martin CSI design, fabricate, install, and service custom-made machinery, assembly lines, and control panels for manufacturers. Yes, it's as technical, complicated, and advanced as it sounds!

But one of the keys to their long-term Success is not.

Joe Martin, the Founder of Martin CSI, spent a day with me, sharing the stories of the company's journey, as well as the important life lessons he's learned along the way.

One of his statements grabbed my attention: "John, there's no such thing as work/life balance."

I've heard that term so often in the workplace, that it didn't make sense. He helpfully explained what he meant.

"Work/life balance is impossible to achieve," Joe continued. "There'll be times in our lives when family needs outweigh those at work. And there'll be periods of time when my business requires more. Work/life flow is my goal."

One of Joe's biggest Why's was his family. His wife and children understood that running a company requires more than a 9-5 commitment at times, and they readily supported Joe's dream.

But not at their expense only.

Joe shared that business and family can work well together. Core values, upbringing, work ethic, a sense of community, teamwork, joy of productivity, belonging, and the pursuit of excellence—these experiences can apply to both family and business.

Once Joe knew that his family and business had a healthy working relationship with each other, it became simpler to extend that kind of Win/Win approach to team members as the company grew.

Just like Joe's determination to help his company succeed was driven partially by his desire to provide for his family, he also wanted his employees and company leaders to thrive as the business grew.

Because his core values were non-negotiable, his family, employees, leaders, vendors & suppliers, colleagues, and customers all knew that Joe would come through. He would keep his word no matter what happened in the market, the economy, or through up-and-down business cycles.

Joe made a point to model gratefulness, kindness, and diligence for his children and his team members, knowing that his actions spoke louder than his words. A "healthy" workplace and home required authentic care for others, to the point that revenue was never more important than relationships.

In the negotiations with a prospective customer, one of Joe's skilled engineers was repeatedly patronized and ignored...because she was a woman. After admonishing the business leader that she was an invaluable member of the team, deserving of respect, the unacceptable behavior continued. Without a second thought, Joe turned the prospect away, underlining his commitment to a fair and respectable working environment. The decision cost the company a great deal of money. But it proved to Joe's team that his core values were non-negotiable.

To get an appreciation for the culture Joe and his team have built, check out their fun website: https://martincsi.com/about-us/our-culture

Not a business owner? Good!

Customers and vendors expect business owners and key leaders to act in a certain way. If your current role is not THE owner or THE president of the company, you have an even better opportunity to impact others for good....... if that's one of your Why's. Let me share a powerful tool with you.

When I first began studying the topic of Customer Experience years ago, the very first book I read was written by John DiJulius: *What's the Secret? To Providing a World-Class Customer Experience.* I was hooked! Since then, I've read every single book John has written. I also had the privilege of speaking with him about 5-star Customer Experience and how it should be a core Why for companies of all sizes.

In all of his books, John shares case studies, statistics, and personal stories that absolutely prove the intentional pursuit of excellent customer experience is profitable and sustainable. One ingenious tool he uses all the time to connect with others helps unearth their Why's.

He calls it the F.O.R.D. method, the letters standing for: Family, Occupation, Recreation, and Dreams. Whether John is riding in an Uber, flying on a plane, or talking with attendees at a conference, he uses this approach to learn more about them, to connect with them. He asks questions about where they were raised, if they have family in the area, what they do for a living, what they do for fun, and what dreams they have that they're willing to share. He's taught his children and his team members this tool, as well as the thousands of people who've attended his engaging conferences and the students at his Customer Experience Academy in Cleveland, Ohio. The result?

Real connections. People feel most valued when others take the time to ask well-worded questions and listen to their answers. No pitch, no sales, no angle. We can brighten others' days by genuinely caring about them, even if only for a few minutes.

If adding value to others is a Why for us, it will result in a life full of enjoyable, meaningful conversations at work, at home, in social settings, during travel---anywhere you find people. It's easy to remember, and so much fun to do!

To learn more about John's invaluable Customer Experience training, visit his website: https://thedijuliusgroup.com/project/cx-executive-academy/.

You're a Hero!

Why has Heroism pulled at humanity across the ages? Why does it consume our childhoods, imagination, and entertainment? What is so universal about wanting to be a Hero?

You've probably guessed what I did next. Yep, I went to the dictionary to find out what it meant and what its origins were. Fascinating.

Heroism is not restricted to Hollywood characters, the military, first responders, healthcare providers, or educators. It's far more accessible and achievable than you might think. In fact, it's highly likely that you're pursuing Heroic endeavors right now.

Heroism, it turns out, is simply the pursuit of two ideals: a higher purpose and excellence. Let's unpack each one of these Why's.

A Higher Purpose

Because you've already completed the exercise from earlier in the chapter (you did, right?), you already have identified your deepest Why by asking yourself "Why?" 5 times.

Not only is that your deepest Why, it's most likely your higher purpose as well. My deepest Why comes from my personal faith. This is true of many other people as well. Other examples include: making a difference in the world, saving lives, saving livelihoods, encouraging others, giving people hope, helping others to learn, creating a sense of community, and more.

If you're working at this ideal, you *ARE* being Heroic, at the purest definition. No validation from others is necessary. It's a fact. If something beyond yourself is driving you to work hard, serve others, and get up every morning to take on the day, you *ARE* a Hero.

Yes, there's a catch. "I knew it!" you're probably thinking. But it's not as complicated as you might think. It's simply the second aspect of being Heroic: pursuing Excellence.

Nobility

The actual one-word definition in Merriam-Webster's dictionary was "nobility." Since most civilizations no longer have monarchs as leaders, the idea of nobles is somewhat vague. Thankfully, the dictionary added, "or excellence." Now we're on to something!

I have yet to encounter a company or a person that said from the very outset, "I'm only here to provide an "okay", "average", "lukewarm", "3-star" experience. And yet, sadly, this is quite often the result we face as customers, co-workers, and leaders.

So what happened? Why do so many people and businesses start off with the best intentions yet end up in average or poor experiences?

This is where the Heroic part comes in.

Heroes all around us are providing 5-star work, service, or care for others **in spite of** how they feel, or what's going on in their lives or happening all around them. **THAT** is Heroism.

When you add value to others in these ways, it's the same as pinning on a cape and flying to the rescue of someone in distress. I would make the case that the everyday Heroics of people we may never meet exceed the Heroism we normally attribute to exceptional people or industries. Why?

Because it's easier to be Heroic in the spotlight. It's easier to be a Hero when it's expected or automatically credited to us. I can testify to that as a veteran of the U.S. Armed Forces.

I'm deeply grateful for the sincere best wishes and thanks from people around the world. There are times, however, where I feel like the phrase, "Thank you for your service" is almost a knee-jerk response. In those cases, I never feel like a Hero, as do most service members.

That's why I believe that there are innumerable people, all around us, that are everyday Heroes, to those people who are **their** Why. They're counting on you to come through. If you don't, no one else will.

Why am I telling you this? Why am I working so hard to help you "get" this? Just like you may have thought you're not a Winner, you've probably also thought that you're not a Hero.

Both are not only likely to be wrong, they're most likely to be true of you as well. Remember I promised you at the very beginning of this book that I would not "spin"---

use magical words or twist meanings---to simply make you feel better about yourself. My Why goes deeper than that. Let me share the story behind my Why.

My Life Purpose--Why I'm here

In May of 2019, I decided to visit an authors' club in the Columbus, Ohio area. After viewing several livestream meetings, it seemed like a good idea to visit in person, to get a feel for the group.

As soon as I walked into the half-lit room, with rows of tables & chairs facing a brightly lit stage, a kind, elderly woman approached me. Remember, I had never been to this meeting in person, so all these people were known to me only through the Internet.

Pat introduced herself, asked for my name, and why I was there. After politely listening to my answer, she surprised me.

"John, I help people discover their life purpose. Would you like to know yours?"

"What the heck," I thought to myself. "Why not?"

When I agreed, she took my hands and said, "We're going to pray together, and when we're done, your life purpose will be revealed to you. Tell me the first word that comes to your mind."

She mentioned a verse in the book of Revelation in the Bible that supported her belief. We prayed together, quite briefly, and then opened our eyes. Just before finishing the prayer, a word flashed into my mind: "Encourager."

"That's your life purpose, John," Pat excitedly affirmed. "That's what you've been put here to do."

It all made sense. Looking back throughout my life, I realized that how people felt was important to me. I vividly recalled multiple scenes of helping sad kids and disappointed adults feel better, cheering them up with kind words and affirmation.

As I matured and became concerned about others more than myself, I found my greatest fulfillment in encouraging others, literally infusing their lives with courage—building them up on truths I identified in their lives.

Just a couple of months after meeting Pat and discovering my life purpose, I received the longest and biggest hug of my life by using that gift.

That same author's club, Igniting Souls, holds an annual conference in the Columbus, Ohio area. On Sunday, the last day of the 3-day event, the speaker was.....Kary Oberbrunner. Yep, the same person you met in Chapter 3. Kary is the founder of Igniting Souls. It was his livestream that led me to Pat Gano and discovering my life purpose.

I remember this scene like it happened yesterday. One of the live exercises was to speak positive words into the lives of the other people at my table. Everyone briefly shared about their lives, and then we went around the table, affirming each other.

The lady immediately to my right spoke directly into my soul, so much so that I wrote it down and carry it with me everywhere I go. She said, "You have deep value and can be the person who smiles to someone and keeps them from going to a dark place. You have saved people without knowing it."

Wow! That was the most powerful experience I've ever had at a conference. I sometimes get chills thinking back to that day.

As we were wrapping up the exercise, I spoke additional encouraging words to her, knowing she was facing a very difficult time in her life. That's when The Hug happened.

Before heading on to different parts of the conference, she pulled me into one of the most loving, grateful, affirming hugs I've ever had, as if she were saying "Thank you" from the bottom of her soul. I KNEW my words had a significant impact on her life.

THAT is why I am here. So when I express that you're a Winner at Life, you're a Hero to those who need you---I mean it from the bottom of my heart. Because my life purpose is to encourage you---to pour courage into your life by identifying what is absolutely true about you. I have nothing to gain personally from sharing these truths with you. This is one way that I carry out the life mission I've been given. That's my Higher Purpose.

What's yours? Do you know what it is? If you do, are you using it often, every day, occasionally, or not as much as you'd like?

If you know your life purpose, use it.

If you want to know it, do this: ask several people you respect---who have nothing to gain from giving you feedback---what qualities they see in your life. The one identified most by all of them, that may very well be your Life Purpose. Then look back through your life. Is there a pattern? Have you used this talent/skill/ability/gifting before?

Odds are that you're making a difference in others' lives; you just may not have thought about it before. There's no better time than Today to ask others and infuse courage into your life. If I was sitting next to you, I would! Do it Today! The people depending on you need to benefit from your unique purpose.

One cool footnote---Pat Gano wrote her first book in her 80's. That's right! I met her when she was 87. Pat is still going strong today, helping others identify their Life Purpose. Her book is entitled *The 7 Languages of Heaven*. Of course, I got an autographed copy! It's available on Amazon, and definitely worth getting if you believe your personal faith has you on this earth for a Higher Purpose.

You're Outstanding!

Okay, maybe very few people (besides your grandmother!) have told you something like this. But that's the literal definition for Excellence. When you stand out, you are achieving Excellence. Simple as that.

It's not as hard to stand out in a good way, I've found. In almost every career role I've held, I've advanced within those companies—in responsibilities, income, and leadership roles. When I was younger, others' approval was so important to me that I became somewhat of a chameleon—adapting to whatever I thought the people in charge wanted me to act, be, do, or say.

Now that I've matured and grown in healthy self-confidence, I approach everything with the same mantra: "My very best work, everywhere I work, will always work out for the good of others and myself."

In his remarkable book, *Excellence* Wins, Horst Schulze, the founder of Ritz Carlton hotels, eloquently stated: "There's always room at the top for excellence."

Good enough, okay, decent, not bad, acceptable—these words don't sit well with me, as do the phrases, "We've always done it this way" or "If it ain't broke, don't fix it"—tragic phrases of mediocrity!

Pursuing excellence has been a core value for me throughout my career. I always ask myself, "How can we do this better?" My standing assumption is that it can **always** be better.

This burning question—how can we do this better?—is at the heart of continuous improvement. People who embrace this life philosophy appreciate the effort and extraordinary attention to detail. Is this what you do?

Are you someone who's bothered by unfinished or sloppy work? Do you put just a few more minutes of effort into something so that you can end the day or wrap up the project feeling good about your work?

That's Excellence. People who live at this level of quality are invaluable. If this describes you, and your motivation is about others, you **are** a Hero, every day.

Happiness or something greater?

The American Declaration of Independence guarantees the right to the **pursuit** of happiness, not happiness itself. One of the keys to true happiness is that it can't be given to you, it can't be bought, and it can't be faked. You must find something greater. I can help you with that!

Happiness is an end result of a fulfilled, content life. We will always be chasing happiness, never quite achieving it if *that* is the end goal.

If a fulfilled life is the goal, then happiness will be a direct by-product. Happiness can be temporary, but fulfillment is long-term and unshakable, no matter the circumstances in our life. Fulfillment is based on tangible, enduring aspects of our lives: relationships, achieved goals, giving to others, efforts outside of ourselves.

There's a big secret to being fulfilled and happy. Would you like to hear it?

The Trust Institute

In November 2021, I attended a healthcare conference in San Diego, California. David Horsager was one of the keynote speakers. David is the founder of The Trust Institute. I highly recommend following him on social media, subscribing to his material, and getting his books. His presentation on earning and keeping trust was powerful.

One stat in particular that he shared has stuck with me all this time. He said the number one attribute that makes people highly trusted and very attractive to others was this big secret.

When you read it, you may think to yourself, "That's it?! That's the key to being happy?!" It's true!

Gratefulness.

People who make gratitude an integral part of their lives are more happy, more fulfilled, more Successful, more attractive, and more impactful to others.

If you think about it, though, it makes perfect sense. Who would you rather spend time with—someone who constantly complains or someone who is thankful?

One of our Why's should be gratefulness. Gratefulness for the opportunity to Win, for a start. There are places in the world and there have been times in history where--- depending on our gender, the color of our skin, who we were born to, or where we were born, or our education level---we would have been barred from pursuing any opportunity at all.

For most of us reading this book, we have the freedom to pursue our dreams. One of the greatest reasons why we should strive to Win even more, is *because* we have the freedom to do it. I'm definitely grateful for that!

Just 5 years old

That's when it started for me---my love of learning. When I was 5 years old, my parents enrolled me in a charity's reading contest. For every kid's book I completed, read out loud to them, my grandparents and parents donated to the non-profit association to help disabled children.

I still remember that old Polaroid picture of me and my older brother, grinning from ear to ear, holding up our gold medals for reading so many books.

I'm deeply grateful to my parents for starting me off on such a lifelong love affair. Yep, I'm a bibliophile and a logophile.

Wait, wait! Before you call the police, Google those 2 words for me. They're not as bad as they sound, I promise you!

I love to read, to learn, to study the meanings and origins of words. Being a bibliophile (book lover) has introduced me to scores of best-selling authors & speakers. I've been coached by some of the most brilliant minds in business, self-improvement, finance, leadership, earning &

keeping trust, relationships, and entrepreneurialism, just to list a few topics.

So many presentations and book ideas have come from studying the meanings, definitions, and origins of words. I find tremendous fulfillment in reframing tired, old paradigms into fresh, life-changing insights through my love of words (being a logophile). That's how this book came to be a reality.

What about you? Do you love to learn? Do you enjoy reading for pleasure and for insight? Are you intrigued by what things mean? That could also be a Why for you. You don't work with your utmost effort just to earn a paycheck. You provide your very best work because you enjoy learning something new.

Not only will a love for learning keep you young, it will also keep you valuable. Have you ever heard of The Curiosity Gap? No? Awesome! Let me tell you about it.

In a couple of the books I've read recently, this Gap came up. Essentially, those who have a Curiosity Gap realize that there will always be information and ideas that they've not yet encountered or explored. People, with this Gap, are always fascinated by new ideas and concepts. It doesn't matter where they encounter these ideas---books, podcasts, speakers, blogs, conversations, etc. An insatiable hunger to know more drives them to ask more questions, do more research, and think more about these topics.

Those who do not possess a hunger to learn display a lack of curiosity. They're satisfied, listen to this, to what **they think they know**. Because they have no desire to learn more, they don't believe there is a Gap. They're either satisfied with their current level of knowledge or falsely believe they know all there is to know on that topic.

Here's the tragic irony.

Those who love to learn realize that there will **always** be a learning gap. They will never know all there is to know on any topic, let alone all topics. And this drives them to learn more, never satisfied with their current level of understanding.

In stark contrast, those who are satisfied with what they **think** they know, a.k.a. "know-it-alls" (I used to be one of those [cringe]), do not see the yawning knowledge gap the size of the Grand Canyon right in front of them.

The sad result is those who would benefit the most from a life devoted to learning, deprive themselves and those around them. The wonderful blessing of learning is reserved for the hungry, who choose to learn their whole lives, enriching their life and those around them.

Which one are you?

Not only does this Why bless you and those around you, it's one of the most powerful Secrets to a Winning Life.

The one who is always learning will always be in a much better position to seize opportunity and make the most of it. Always.

Whether you like to read a book, listen to podcasts, or spend time with learned, respectable circles of influence, add one, several, or all these forms of learning. Start learning, and Winning, today!

What kind of electricity are you?

One of my favorite presentations, and the topic of a future book (of course!), is entitled "Your 3 Most Precious Resources." You'd be right if you guessed that Time was one of those treasures. But surprisingly, Money is not. Without giving away the entire book, let me share another one on that list: Energy.

We only have so much of this to go around. Whether it's short-term energy (for the day) or long-term energy (to achieve big goals & dreams), it's limited. People directly impact our energy levels. So do you.

There are 3 possibilities: an energy giver (positive), pleasant (neutral) or an energy drain (negative). To be clear, I'm not talking about personalities—extrovert, introvert, etc. Putting it simply: when people spend time with you, how do they feel after?

If you don't know, you should ask someone you trust, who has no reason to flatter you or sugar-coat their answer. Truth over feelings really matters on this one! Truth tellers who genuinely care for you—you need to ask them this question.

For much of my life, I was focused on making people feel good so that they would like me. My best interest was at the heart of all the kind things I would say to others. It wasn't conscious; I wasn't trying to manipulate them. In sincere self-reflection, I realized that I was constantly seeking the approval of others, with the roots of that longing going all the way back to childhood. Perhaps you can identify with that.

Interestingly, the moment my focus shifted to my life purpose—encouraging others—that's when I began to add value to others, to brighten their days, to encourage them. I also grew in confidence, self-worth, and gratefulness.

Here's the Winning Secret I learned: Before I could fulfill my life purpose and add value to others, I had to genuinely be fully concerned about **them**, **their** wellbeing, **their** confidence, **their** self-worth. When I did that, I received those same things, not because they were my focus but because they were my reward, my blessing.

There's a spiritual principle that says it's more blessed to give than to receive. Too often, this is assumed to be talking about money. While money is one way to give, it's been proven that it has the least amount of lasting impact. It's far better to give love, kindness, gratitude, wisdom, affirmation, recognition, and encouragement than money. And the impact of those things literally changes lives. It changed mine. And that sweet lady that gave me the biggest hug of my life. And all the people I've coached, mentored, and led.

The same is true of you. If you've given these blessings to others, you're already Winning at Life in one of the most precious ways possible. Adding value to others, genuinely loving them, IS Winning, in the way that matters most. When my time on earth is done, I will not care about the dollars in my bank account. I will have peace knowing I've made a difference in so many lives and fulfilled my life purpose.

My Deepest Why—Winning Secret #8

"I thought we already identified that your deepest Why was to encourage others, John?" No, that's my life purpose, but not my deepest Why.

Like many other remarkable people in my life, my deepest Why comes from my personal faith. My deepest Why will always come back to this: glorifying the One Who made me.

That's why I encourage others. That's why I want to add value to others. That's why I love to learn. That's why I want to do my very best work, every time. That's why I'm blessed to provide for my loved ones. That's why I'm grateful and look forward to the fresh opportunity in a new day.

That's my deepest Why, and I believe it's also the deepest Why for many reading this book. And rightly so.

Why?

Our toddler went through this well-known phase of asking that one-word question, more as a knee-jerk, automatic response than a genuine thirst for knowledge! Nevertheless, there were times where he really meant it— he wanted to understand something better.

It's not surprising that this chapter is one of the largest in the book. The "Why" question is built into us, hardwired. Sadly, over time or because of tragic life experiences, the thirst for knowledge is lost.

Ask yourself "Why", as many times as it takes, to be encouraged, to identify where you're already Winning at life, and to perhaps rekindle the passion for your deepest Why.

Take time today to re-discover your Why's. You'll be glad you did!

Winning Secrets: Why and Who For
My Menu

_____

_____

_____

_____

_____

_____

Chapter 6

Who With and Who From

"You will never outperform your inner circle."

John Wooden

Jim Rohn famously said that we're the average of the 5 people we spend the most time with. Yikes!

Take a quick survey of the 5 people you spend the most time within a week. Are some changes in order?

How many people in your circles believe that failure is a tool to Success? How many believe that Winning at life **does not** come from comparing themselves to others? Who in your circle believes in **you**, not your circumstances, income, or degrees?

Who we spend our time with, matters. It matters a bunch! When I was a kid, I heard a couple of sayings over and over. Perhaps you have. "Bad company corrupts good morals." And "Birds of a feather, flock together."

Think of the people around you as your environment. We all know that a healthy atmosphere in nature is better for all living things. How much more so the mindsets, attitudes, thoughts, goals, and dreams of the people around us?

Start thinking about your circle that way: are they refreshing or polluting? Are they like the Rocky Mountains in Colorado or more like downtown Los Angeles on a hot and humid day?

More to the point, which one are you? Which one am I?

Leadership

John Maxwell wisely said that everything rises and falls on leadership. Agreed! Whether we have any input as to who the leaders are around us or not, it makes a great difference who's leading in our career world.

Joe Martin, the founder of Martin CSI (we shared his story in the previous chapter), cited one key leader in our discussion—Bill. Bill was one of his first hires, a decision that would prove to be invaluable over time.

Joe entrusted the technical side of the business to Bill, having full trust in him because of his honesty and accessibility. Joe knew Bill would be committed for the long haul. This freed Joe to focus on growing the business and hiring more people to support that growth.

But trust was a two-way street for Bill & Joe. Bill had worked with Joe before Joe left to start his own company. Bill knew Joe to be grateful, recognizing people's efforts, and including everyone. Joe was quick to offer help with work needs or family needs when they arose. Bill said Joe was always supportive, especially during his transition from the previous company that offered more stability. Bill chose to leave that "secure" role for a somewhat risky opportunity with Joe because his old work environment was toxic. He was completely confident that the culture at Martin CSI would be healthy and rewarding.

Like Joe, Bill shared common values on family, work, relationships, and how business gets done. Mutual respect; The Golden Rule; fix the issue, not the blame; work/life flow and earning trust with honesty & quality—it's easy to see why their working relationship has lasted so long and been so Successful.

Luck or something else?

Did Joe and Bill just get lucky? Did they just happen to work at the same company before Martin CSI was created? Or was something greater at work?

Before you accuse me of getting all mystical on you, I promise this will have *WAY* more to do with proven science than potent mushrooms!

The Law of Attraction, or Personal Magnetism, as I call it—I used to think it was a bunch of baloney [poor baloney, always getting slammed for no good reason! What's up with that?!]. Turns out, I was wrong, dead wrong. [Again, another poor word choice, obviously, because I wouldn't be writing this book if I had literally been dead wrong. Ah, well.]

Call it whatever you want, but it's undeniable that certain people have an irresistible attractiveness about them. Thank goodness this has nothing to do with good looks or I'd always come up short!

This has more to do with personality—their smile, their energy, their outlook on life, their goals & dreams, their authentic desire to add value to others—all this comes through.

Just like magnetism, we can see the effect without actually seeing the force. Do you know people like this? Not the born salespeople that attract others' attention to sell them something.

I'm talking about the people who you spot in the middle of a crowd, and you think to yourself, "I need to talk to that person." And when you do, your life is better because of it. Let me share just such a person with you.

She had "It"

In 2019, I resolved to attend as many after-hours business networking events as possible. I had just published my first book on world-class customer service and was eager to add value to small & mid-size companies in the world of customer experience. Multiple mentors told me that in-person networking was an excellent way to build Win/Win relationships and get my name out there.

At one event, the venue was small, and the place was packed. Conversations verged on yelling matches to be heard over the dull roar of so many people speaking in such a crowded space. As I scanned the attendees, that's when I saw her.

Long, dark hair, stylish eyeglasses, a quiet smile, intelligent, friendly—Brittany Dixon had a different look than most people in the room, so I struck up a conversation. At that time, she was working on growing her consulting business. She, too, saw in-person networking as a great way to connect with prospective clients or centers of influence. Sounds like just about everyone else in the room, right?

True. Except for one thing....

She asked great questions about me, what I was looking for from attending the event. And she was genuinely interested in my answers because she asked well-worded, follow up questions. Her positive attitude, enthusiasm, and concern for others was obvious.

My experience with her was in stark contrast to most people who rushed through their elevator pitch, handed me their business card, and quickly moved on to the next person. Most people who asked for my business card did not follow up after the meeting, and those who did, simply repeated their pitch and asked who I knew that could use their product or service. Brittany and I scheduled coffee to learn more about each other's endeavors and stay connected.

Years later, Brittany has built a very Successful business, and we still stay in touch. She's one of the few people that has shown genuine, lasting care for what I'm pursuing. THAT's an energy giver.

If you'd like to learn more about her remarkable solutions that give business owners & entrepreneurs their lives back, check out her website and game-changing solutions:

https://bcohq.co/workwithus/.

Speaking of networking

There's one more person I want to share with you, a true energy giver. And that's the person who made my introduction to Brittany Dixon possible—Chris Borja.

If you met Chris when I did, you would never imagine that, for a good part of his life, he was a shy, quiet introvert. Dublin Area Networking Group, or DANG for short, was the attention-grabbing name of Chris' in-person, weekly networking group, held at different venues in the central Ohio area. Chris was a confident, polished speaker, smoothly hosting the meetings, sharing excellent tips on how to network effectively, and personally connecting professionals who shared complementary pursuits. But it's his personal journey leading up to our first meeting that's extraordinary.

Early on in his career, Chris quickly moved into retail management due to his professionalism, polite nature, and commitment to following guidelines. The strong work ethic he learned from his father enabled him to move up quickly in an industry that was notorious for high turnover, poor service, and challenging customers. His corner office ambitions looked to be coming together in retail....until his life took an unexpected turn.

Chris joined a few colleagues to invest in real estate. All was going well, until the 2008 subprime mortgage fiasco. Not only did everything go south for the group of investors, his partners took advantage of Chris' honesty by leaving him to take the brunt financially and legally. This plunged Chris and his family into a very difficult time. But in every challenge, for those who choose to focus on taking the next best step and overcome, there's always a major life lesson or two, as well as the opportunity to learn who your true friends really are.

Not only did Chris choose to serve others while going through the toughest time for him and his young family, his true friends made cross-country trips to support him in person, vouching for his character. It was a very difficult lesson, but Chris learned to identify people of unquestionable integrity and the clues to spot the phonies.

With a new beginning in central Ohio, Chris decided to use his newly discovered strength of building & keeping quality relationships as his next career pursuit.

Through a process of trial & error that spanned several years, Chris diligently fine-tuned a Win/Win approach to effective professional networking. When I met Chris, he was just a couple of years from a major breakthrough. And, like before, it came during a time of difficulty. But not for him.

With the onset of the pandemic in 2020, Chris' in-person networking events ground to a halt. Chris attributes much of his Success to Grit—persevering on a proven idea no matter what obstacles get thrown in the way. And persevere he did.

Chris created a virtual solution so that professionals could still network socially and for business growth, while also offering virtual events on a remarkably engaging platform.

While many professionals put business pursuits on hold, Chris went on the offense, partnering with emerging brands like COHatch, Igniting Souls, and SpeakX, to name a few. The result?

Multiple national & global virtual events, virtual & in-person networking across 6 continents, 29 countries, and over 275,000 people impacted. Now THAT's Winning at life!

When I sat down with Chris through two interviews, I was struck by how genuine and authentic he remains, despite his well-deserved Success. The biggest takeaway for me was Who With—Who were the people that Chris worked With, partnered With, and served With to achieve his goals and dreams.

Who do you have in your inner circle? Are they the quality of people that will support YOU, not your ambitions or endeavors, but YOU. Life doesn't go by the script we write for it, hardly ever. The people you can trust unquestionably become a Key Secret to Winning at Life.

Your Inner Circle—Winning Secret #9

Take stock of who your closest personal and professional relationships are. It can mean the difference between Winning at Life or surviving. Don't take for granted the diamonds in your life, and don't trust the posers (the cubic zirconium's).

Do It Now: Make a list of the closest friends and relatives you have, the ones you could trust with your life, your money, your most intimate relationships & experiences. If you feel like your list is shorter than it should be, learn to network effectively, add mentors to your life, and visit groups that are led by thought leaders you respect & admire. Happy with your list or feel like you have knowledge or expertise to share? Start your own group!

If you want to learn more about Chris Borja's highly effective networking solutions and his virtual events, visit his website: chrisborja.com.

Who Without

Toxic relationships—just like a drop of poison in a pure glass of water, the impact can be fatal, to your goals & dreams, healthy relationships, work environment, and home life. They can negatively affect every area of your life.

We should work hard to keep the "diamonds"— trustworthy people—in our lives. Even more importantly, we should identify the toxic people we should severely limit or remove from our lives altogether.

Joe Martin of Martin CSI shared a story that underlined this priority so well. One major prospective client repeatedly patronized and ignored a female sales engineer on Joe's team.

After multiple warnings went unheeded, Joe refused to do business with the man's company, bringing the loss of millions of dollars in revenue. Why?

Because treating all his team members with respect was a non-negotiable value for Joe. No amount of business was worth sacrificing a core value. Not only did this decision underline Joe's commitment to the declined customer, it proved to Joe's team that their wellbeing came first, not the business.

Multiple times, I've chosen to remove toxic relatives from my family's life because of the loss of peace, the stealing of precious time, the constantly negative attitudes, the cutting words, and the refusal to learn from others. While that has limited relationships with other relatives as a by-product, the emotional and spiritual health of my family is stronger than ever.

Set boundaries and protect them.

Often, the most toxic people in our lives are those who are closest to us. Choose the ones you will make time for, the ones you will keep in your life. View your time and your energy as invaluable, limited precious resources that cannot be squandered. You cannot have a Winning Life while allowing toxic people to drain you.

Think of a highly Successful life as a bucket full of water. The more intact your bucket is, the more full your life is. The more holes, cracks, and drains you have, the less full-filling your life becomes.

Who With and Who Without—figure this out now.

You do not want to continue down this path for several years, only to look back and regret not taking decisive action to protect yourself, your goals & dreams, and your loved ones. If you have Olympic-sized goals & dreams, don't let toxic naysayers sap the energy & focus you need to achieve them. Be sure to include the coaches, friends, and colleagues who will help you cross the finish line and celebrate with you when you do!

Do It Now: Make a list of people who drain your time, energy, finances, or happiness. Limit or eliminate these relationships from your life. You cannot pour from an empty cup.

Who From

Quick question for you: the person who impacted your life the most, who comes to mind? For Sharon, it was her father.

Born in China to a professor at Peking University, Sharon remembers vividly how the culture changed, from shared Success in a healthy capitalistic environment to the loss of personal freedom, innovation, and hope for a better future. Sharon entered the world at the eve of the darkest period in Chinese history, the beginning of the Cultural Revolution.

Despite growing persecution for his personal values, Sharon's father poured heavily into her life, even down to the names he gave her: "Water Lily" and "Dawn". He told her that the most beautiful flower can come from the muddiest ponds, and that Hope comes after the darkest part of the day.

As Sharon talked about her growing up years with me, I was moved by her gratitude and determination despite those difficult years. When Sharon earned her U.S. citizenship, that Grateful Grit drove her to build & sell her own jewelry business. She believes that Grit always tops talent in countries with abundant opportunities. After selling her business, she pursued a brand-new career as a financial advisor, achieving notable Success to this day.

Sharon and I talked for hours; it was fascinating to hear her life unfold. Full honesty—I was convicted as I realized that I had often allowed excuses to limit my potential at times, especially before my "Aha Moment" that led to the research for this book. Just as Sharon learned from her father, I came away from my time with her with much wisdom and insight. Here were my top takeaways from my time with Sharon.

1) **No matter where we are in our journey through life, we must always receive constructive criticism, from those Who truly care for us.**

In my younger days, I often bristled at the idea that I needed to improve. How dare they! Didn't they know I knew all there was to know at 21 years of age!!

Funny sidebar: reminds me of a humorous anecdote by Mark Twain. He said, "When I was 17, I thought my father was the dumbest man on the face of the earth. At 25, I was amazed to discover how much he had learned in 8 years!" Touché, Mark, Touché!

Notice Sharon said **_Constructive_** criticism. Like a skilled surgeon deftly cuts away the dangerous cells and leaves the healthy ones intact, the truth tellers in our lives help us gain a competitive advantage by contributing to our continuous improvement.

John Maxwell has stated that he consistently asks his team, "How can we do this better?" The standing assumption should be that we can always improve. Just like riding a bicycle, the day we stop improving, is the day we fall on our face. John Maxwell said, "The greatest danger is Today's Success. What got you here, won't get you there." Ask for, assess, glean, and apply wise input from trusted mentors.

2) A coachable attitude is critical to achieve more.

It's one of my non-negotiables. When I am assessing whether to work with someone, to attach my name, personal brand, and well-earned reputation to them, they must have a hunger to learn, a teachable, coachable spirit. The greatest athletes in the world rely on coaches to help them achieve their potential. We who desire to Win at Life must do the same.

News flash: Those of us who are Winning at Life **already have** mentors and/or coaches. Coaches are paid professionals, while mentors are paying it forward to honor a mentor who did the same for them, at no charge.

Whether highly Successful people have a coach, a mentor or both, no accomplished coach or mentor will ever take on a client or mentee who does not have a teachable spirit.

If you want to achieve your potential, if you want to Win at Life, you must be willing to receive and implement wise input from respectable people in your life.

Great advice is only great when it's applied.

It's like sunken treasure just under the surface of the water, but the people in the boat don't feel like diving down to get it. Absurd, isn't it? Don't pass over the wealth of wise counsel.

3) Do not sacrifice your values

Be selective about which kind of Successful people you receive constructive criticism from. Success at any price is not Winning at Life. It might be Winning at income or bragging rights or building an ego, but it is NOT Winning at Life. We will go into great detail on what the ultimate Winning at Life looks like in the last chapter.

Who From—the character, caliber, and values of the highly Successful counselor matters. Jim Rohn once said that we are the average of the 5 people with whom we spend the most time. Evaluate this regularly!

All the highly Successful people I interviewed shared a common trait—they were all transparently honest about where they messed up, what they learned from, and who they discovered could not be trusted. This may seem to go against the spirit of this book that is intentionally positive. Hear me out.

I'm positively certain that we learn the most from what did not go according to plan, who to avoid, and what to do differently next time. Every person I spoke with said something to this effect. The wisest question I've learned to ask is: "What should I avoid doing?" "Who should I avoid working with?"

It's far easier to never go down an unwise path than to put in the grueling work to return to the right one.

4) Inspiration is the fuel for our Motivation

Just like Sharon, I have a regular habit of reading, following, and digesting positive, uplifting content across multiple media platforms. Why?

Because everyday life is full of the opposite.

We're bombarded with negative news, events, difficulties, challenges, and unexpected losses or pains. In order to keep a healthy perspective, we must have a steady, intentional diet of the 4 L's: Laughter, Love, Life, and Learning.

Laughter truly is the best medicine, so I watch my favorite comedians a little every day.

Seeing parents Love their children or families Loving on their pets blesses my soul, lifts my spirit. So I watch videos that fill my heart with Love.

To see others living their Life to the fullest— adventures, travel, promotions, relocations and pursuing Big Hairy Audacious Goals—these stories inspire me, whether I know these people or not.

When others share what they are Learning with me, on any topic, of any age, I love it! My mind is like a sponge, eager to Learn something new. Every day should be filled with the quest to add some new insight to our life that we did not possess when the day began.

If you're doing one, some, or all of these 4 things, you already **are** Winning at Life....big time! Keep it up!!

5) Lastly, **we must be truth seekers**

Most of my life, I sought to find absolute truth, in my faith, in my relationships, in my pursuits, in my learning. While there are some non-negotiables that have never changed for me, much of what I thought was true turned out to be somewhat, mostly, or all untrue over time, as I matured & learned through life experiences.

At first, this bothered me. How was I to lead others, especially my loved ones, if I did not know truth? What if I was leading them astray, down a wrong path, even with the best of intentions?

I learned to say this simple phrase, "My working understanding is..." or "my current belief is..." Because life is constantly changing, I found it was unwise to stake an immovable position on an opinion or understanding.

"So we shouldn't have strong beliefs or non-negotiable values, John?"

Heck, no! My personal faith has held a number of unshakeable truths and values close to my heart for my entire life. Living out those values has proven to be more challenging than I realized it would be. That doesn't mean those values are wrong. It often meant that I was not applying them correctly in my life and towards others.

While Excellence is the goal in everything I do, the outcome will never be perfection.

Remember that sign in my client's meeting room: "Progress is the goal, not perfection." My understanding and application of values and truth is always maturing, improving, growing. Here's the takeaway:

We must do the best job we can, with the understanding that the person we're most accountable for is us, ourselves. How we live out our values and faith, that's how we Win at Life. As a parent, my ultimate goal is to help guide my children to determine these things for themselves, not simply copying my beliefs and values.

The same is true for you. I desire for you to take and apply what speaks to your heart and mind from this book. The number of ideas is not as important as the **application** of those new ideas that speak to you, that intersect with your values and beliefs. That's when I have succeeded as an author, as a truth teller in your life.

Proximity ≠ Relationship

Who are your truth tellers? Before you answer, let me state that these do not have to be people you have met face-to-face, or at all. Huh?

For one year, I kept a personal commitment to read and notate one physical book per week. Most of those leading authors I've never met and may never speak with in-person. But I learned a great deal from them.

Friendships can be the same way. My family has lived outside Columbus, Ohio for over 10 years—same property, same neighbors. But I barely know their names, let alone the names of their kids and grandkids or what they do for a living.

Are these people mean and nasty? Not at all. Did my wife and I go out of our way to ignore them? Nope.

At the same time, I have ongoing conversations with people literally on the other side of the world. I know what's going on with their family, their work, and their hobbies.

Proximity does not equal relationship.

If you're working intentionally (or definitely will be, now that you read this chapter!) to step up your circle of influencers, don't feel like you have to find these people in the flesh. You absolutely do not.

Take a quick look back to the top of the last page: "The amount of ideas are not as important as the **application** of those new ideas that speak to you, that intersect with your values and beliefs."

And I meant that! Your truth tellers do not matter at all if they're sitting across the table from you at the local coffee shop, if they're a head-and-shoulders person virtually meeting on Zoom, or the author of a book that resonates with you.

Ideas are worthless.... without execution. Better to implement the proven ideas of just one truth teller/virtual coach/best-selling author than 10 in-person influencers whose ideas just gather dust on the shelf.

Action. You must believe in the advice and take action.

Only then will Who From become a powerful Winning Secret that will help you Win More at Life.

Saved the best for last

I really did! This last Winning Secret, when diligently applied, will not only help you Win More at Life, it will also lead you into one of the most fulfilling, rewarding journeys you could possibly imagine.

How about *that* for a teaser?! Write down your action steps from this chapter and join me in the next one. You will be SO glad you did!

Winning Secrets: Who With and Who From

My Menu

_____

_____

_____

_____

_____

_____

Chapter 7

Win/Win

"Win-Win is a belief in the Third Alternative.
It's not your way or my way;
it's a better way, a higher way."
Stephen Covey

THE Winning Secret

I know, I know. SO many books, courses, presentations, conferences, and TV programs promise they have THE insight to Winning. I'm not so stuck on myself that I would think I have the market cornered on the #1 secret to Winning at Life.

Let me phrase it this way: after discovering What Winning at Life is, the Secret I'm about to share with you takes that insight and exponentially increases its impact.

Why? Because this Secret goes way beyond just you and just me. It impacts others.

Win/Win—Winning Secret #10

I was ticked off! "How could he talk to me like that?! He's the one who asked me the question in the first place!"

Who was this guy that was SO rude to me? And why did he feel like he could talk to me that way?

I asked for it; that's a pretty good place to start. A little background might be helpful for you?

If someone were to measure Winning at Life by the following achievements, you'd probably agree they had Won largely at life:

- happy marriage to the same woman for many years
- grown, Successful children
- respected leader in his church
- multiple businesses started, grown, and sold
- center of influence for thousands of entrepreneurs and business owners
- living out his personal commitment to strategically share a significant chunk of his annual income every year

- athletics coach, who teaches character and skills
- devoted friend
- Veteran of the United States Marine Corps

Uh, yeah!! That's what I would definitely call Winning at Life, too!

Chaz, the person I just outlined, wasn't being rude to me. He was being direct. He was being helpfully honest with his feedback when I poorly and sloppily shared my business idea with him.

Chaz firmly believes in helping budding entrepreneurs gain clarity in their ideas, messaging, marketing, and proposals. Why? To quote Donald Miller, "Clarity attracts; confusion repels." If I couldn't clearly explain my business solution and its UVP (Unique Value Proposition) to Chaz, there was NO WAY I would be able to share it with a prospective client either.

Chaz has devoted his life to impacting others. The short list I shared with you on the previous page is proof of that. I had the privilege of spending time with him to glean his Win/Win insights. So here are the Top 7!

1) The #1 attractive quality in people

In the fall of 2021, I had the privilege of hearing David Horsager, Founder of the Trust Institute, speak live at a healthcare conference in San Diego, in November. Glorious weather! (Especially for someone from central Ohio!) David said that studies showed the Number 1 attribute for people with attractive personalities was....

Gratefulness.

Not only do grateful people give energy to others (versus being an "energy vampire" as they're so lovingly called!), but they're more trustworthy because of their intentional pursuit of being thankful.

Chaz and I share the daily priority of choosing gratefulness. I start my day with 3 fresh "Grattitudes", as I call them. Chaz focuses daily on being thankful. That's not always easy, with all the challenges that life throws at us.

For me and Chaz, this is one place where our personal faith comes in. You see, there's a verse in the Bible that says to be thankful IN all things. Not FOR all things. Big difference!

When I was younger, I was the eternal optimist— rainbows and unicorns, rose-colored glasses, the whole deal. I needed a helpful dose of reality to be able to empathize with others. My wife was so helpful for me to grow beyond that over-simplified "everything's gonna be okay" attitude that ignored the challenges.

A grateful person who is optimistic AND realistic would say, "This is tough, not fun right now. But I'm grateful for what I have, and I'm confident we'll figure out a solution." Both—grateful AND optimistic.

2) Giving IS Getting

This saying is often used to compel people to give beyond what they feel comfortable with, most often to people who only have self-serving agendas---TV preachers and their kind. But that's not what Chaz was talking about, and his life proves it.

Here's an excellent example. One of his life goals is to grow his income streams to the point that he can give away half of his income to people, causes, and businesses he believes in. And the same for his time. His goal is 20% of his time in his businesses and 80% to others.

For most of my adult life, my main reason for gaining wealth was to live comfortably. Yes, I was going to give to others. But that was more like a line item in my budget rather than a life goal that drove me to increase my wealth so I could grow my giving and impact.

But it's not just about money for Chaz and the other highly Successful people I spoke with. It involved their most important resource—their time.

They view time as their most precious asset. It's finite, going to run out someday, and they only have 24 hours of it per day. I deeply appreciated their commitment to giving away AND guarding their time.

Jim Collins once wrote, "We must say "No" to the Good in order to say "Yes" to the Great." Preach it!!

This was a common priority for the leaders I interviewed as well as the numerous biographies and profiles I studied of highly Successful people.

Remember Trayvon Brommell, the Olympic sprinter in Chapter 1? How many Good things do you think he said "No" to, in order to pursue his Olympic dreams? Quite a few, I'm sure. As he lined up for the final race in Rio for the Men's Olympic 100-meter dash, do you think those "No's" were worth it? For sure!

What about you? What about your Big Hairy Audacious Goals? What should you say "Yes" to, and what should you be saying "No" to?

In order to make Giving a central part of your life AND achieve your BHAG's, we MUST regularly say "NO!" to the Good things that will delay us or keep us from achieving Great things.

3) Gravitation

A fancy word for Attraction or Magnetism, I had to find a word that started with the letter "G" to keep my alliteration addiction alive!

A common trait of Chaz and others is their appeal to others. So many people want to learn from them, ask them questions, spend time with them, gain their input/influence/friendship, that they must often refer to Insight #2: learning to say "No" to the requests that are not a Best use of their precious time.

It's ironic that the more influence you have, the more selective you need to be about how you invest that time & influence. I have wanted to add value to others ever since I began reading John Maxwell in my early 20's.

But influence doesn't automatically come with a title, a leadership role, or being in front of others. I know this firsthand.

Many of my career steps have been in leadership roles, but that did not mean I was making a difference in the lives of those around me. Now, I regularly have people requesting my time or suggesting I meet with someone to help them. What changed?

Number 1, just like Chaz and others, we genuinely cared about others' Success more than our own. Seriously, it's that simple. And it's also not that simple. Hang on, hang on—I'm not insane. Hear me out.

Just because someone **says** they want to help others doesn't mean that they're sincere (no strings attached, no selfish ask lurking just behind the surface helpfulness----you know who I'm talking about!). Along with sincerity, there also must be capacity to give.

I had a great deal of maturing, life lessons, personal experiences, and relationships to navigate in order to accumulate substance that could bless others.

And I had to get out of my own way.

Yep! I thought I was a pretty big deal when I was in my 20's and 30's! Turns out......not so much. Not at all, really!

I was so anxious to prove that I was helpful, wise, and resourceful that I undermined my own authenticity. And I'm not alone in that.

So many of the people I spoke with shared that they had to learn how to grow in humble confidence to lead & influence others versus acting like they had all the answers. It made all the difference in the world for them and for me. I guarantee it will for you, too.

So before working **so hard** to make a difference in others' lives, spend some time---as much time as it takes--- with yourself and a trusted mentor, to grow into the person who can attract & serve others. It's worth your time, I promise!

4) Ground, common, that is!

For too much of my life, it was more important to be right than to discover what was right, what was true. My opinion mattered more than the facts—true story! My longsuffering brothers can testify that I would argue to the death (the death of happiness and reason!) that I was right on something that was clearly not true, wrong, or foolish. Unfortunately, this immaturity carried through to my adult life, but, even worse, the mask of Knowing It All (yep, I was one of *those!*) was polished with a smile and the desire to be liked by others.

I was a likeable chameleon. If we agreed, we would be best friends. Woe to the truth tellers, truth seekers, and presenters of facts & information that seemed to oppose my unshakable, unquestionable vast accumulation of knowledge! I literally cringe internally when I reflect on all those years of wasted opportunities to learn, grow, mature, and give a listening ear to others.

Common Ground. What do we both agree on? For too long, I believed that being open-minded meant going along with anything that someone else said—no reasoning, logic, or research required, like a screen door on a submarine, letting anything and everything in as truth or facts. Because of my own beliefs and how I was raised, I perceived being reasonable as being weak-minded, susceptible to those who would try to trick me into believing a falsehood or a tall tale.

Thankfully, through maturity, marriage, parenting, mentorship, and some tough times, I've learned that it's far more rewarding to discover what we have in common than to assume how different we are. Assumptions about others is laziness. Working to understand and reason together is genuinely caring about the other person more than ourselves.

In order to give to others, we must be willing to give our time and attention to them. I discovered that one of the most powerful, loving actions I can do is to actively listen to others. A sincere fascination with others' stories, journeys, ideas, and dreams proves that we truly care about them.

Whether I agree fully, somewhat, or not at all with them—that's not important. When people know that I care about them enough to listen well and ask well-worded questions, *THAT* is all important.

John Maxwell's book, Good Leaders Ask Great Questions, is a favorite of mine for that reason. One concept I always remember is this:

The quality of the answer depends on the quality of the question. The better questions we ask, the better answers we get.

Surface questions are nothing but mindless muscle memory of the tongue: "How are you doing?" *EVERYBODY* asks that! Not me. "How is your day going?"—that's what I ask, and I genuinely mean it. How do I show that? If their day is going well, I'm happy for them. If they're having a tough or busy day, I thank them for helping me, serving me, or ask what they have to look forward to later.

Try it. The next time you're served at a restaurant, gas station, or grocery store, ask them how their day is going and follow up that question with a kind, grateful, or empathetic response. It only takes a few seconds. I ***guarantee*** you'll be a day brightener for them, and one of the very few people who genuinely cared for them.

Making a difference in others' lives does not start by being a coach, mentor, leader, or icon. It's who we are, a part of our daily lives as we interact with others....or it's not.

Common ground is best found in the everyday, not the stage, board room, public cause, or media outlets.

Feel stuck? Or not sure where to start? My fellow Customer Experience expert, John DiJulius, has an excellent tool for you: F.O.R.D.

No! I have NOT sold out to the automaker with the blue oval by including a not-so-subtle advertisement in this book,

I promise! Here's John's method of engaging others, building common ground:

F: Family. Ask about their family. Where are they originally from? Do they have family in the area? Is there a big family event coming up? Trust me. People will know if you're genuinely interested in them or phishing for information.

O: Occupation. What do they do for a living? (If it's not perfectly obvious what they do! Come on, people...work with me here! ☺) If what they're currently doing is not a typical full-time career, ask what their dream job would be. You get the idea!

R: Recreation. What do they do for fun? They used to be called Hobbies, when I was a kid. I don't hear that word used much anymore, so I know I'm dating myself a little bit here. My wife says I use old-fashioned words all the time. Maybe stick with, "What do you do for fun?" (Unless they look as old or older than me (39-ish ☺), then feel free to use the ancient word, "Hobbies.")

D: Dreams. Yep. If money doesn't matter, what's your dream? What would you love to do? It's so cool to see how people light up when you genuinely ask this question.

At first, I thought it might feel a little intrusive to ask someone about their dreams. Nope! I've never had someone say, "Back off, weirdo! That's too personal!" They always share with me what they're working on, what they wish they could do, what they want to do & aren't sure if they'll get to.

Very few tell me that they're living their dream. Most often, this question re-ignites an interest, sometimes a passion, to go after that dream again.

Aren't those excellent questions?! It only takes one of those to show you care. If you have enough time to ask all 4, I guarantee you'll have made a difference in their life. Even if you never see that person again, the impact you made on them could change their life.

One thing's for sure: asking these questions to care for others---it will definitely change your life!

5) Group it up!

As cool as energetic people are, synergetic people are incredible! When I discovered this cool word years ago, it transformed my approach to leadership, teamwork, and relationships. Why? It's the result of Win/Win collaboration. Synergy is combined energy. Here's a great word picture for you......

Draft horses---Belgians, Clydesdales, Percherons, Shires, etc.---massive, powerfully majestic animals. A single draft horse can pull an incredible 8,000 pounds! 4 tons!! But as cool as that number is, check this out.

Two draft horses.... guess what they can pull?

24,000 pounds!! That's right, 12 tons, 3 times the weight of an individual horse.

THAT'S synergy.

That's the power of working with like-minded, abundance-minded, others-focused people. And for the right people, the reward they receive from working with others is all the motivation they need. That's one of the character qualities of Chaz that drew me, and keeps drawing others, to him. It's not a show, it has no ulterior or self-serving motives.

Chaz, and those committed to a Win/Win life of synergy, bless others, and are richly blessed in return.

Hang on a sec....... this is NOT a health/wealth, get-rich-quick scheme. People can read through that from a mile away (or a kilometer away for my metric readers! 😊). And isn't that incredibly ironic?!

Those who set out to give, with no strings attached, receive abundantly more in fulfillment, happiness, impact, and sometimes business & revenue than those who give only to get.

And that's another beautiful aspect of Win/Win synergy---you can't fake it.

Authentically caring for & giving to others ALWAYS blesses the giver.

It's so cool!! Try it. I guarantee it will bless your life more than you can imagine. Best part? You don't need money or status or fame to live this kind of life. There will always be people you can bless with this kind of Win/Win giving.

6) Gear up!

Have you ever stepped into the garage of a "gearhead", as they call themselves (or used to, anyways)? Drawer after drawer of hand tools & power tools, stacked on wheels so their massive tool chests can be rolled easily from one mechanical project to the next.

Now, picture yourself as someone who has acquired "tools" as you've lived and learned through life. This is especially true of us who've Successfully navigated the challenges of becoming an adult: maturing from our teenage years (yikes!), through college and our 20's, sometimes with life partners and parenting---typically late 30's early 40's.

Hang on! I'm NOT saying that 20-year-olds have nothing to give to others. I was 20 at one time, whether my children can believe that or not! I did give to others—usually of my time, energy, strong back! and encouragement.

BUT, when I reflect back to those years, I didn't have the invaluable life experiences, quality relationships, and rewarding responsibilities that helped me grow and mature, yet. I had a lot of theory, intelligence, and enthusiasm.

Using our toolbox analogy, I just didn't have a lot of tools to be able to help someone else. I was just starting to collect the tools I needed for my "garage of life." One of the saddest, wasteful things in life is people who have learned so much, yet feel like they're inadequate, unable to give to others. They've allowed damaging, unloving half-truths to affect their adult lives, often burdens they've carried from their childhood.

My Number 1 goal of this book is to help people shed those lies, those hurtful labels, those limiting burdens, and leave them behind for good.

Then, help them pick up what IS true about them, and find ways to use those tools to give to others. The most difficult times in our lives, if they have not hurt us to the point of being unable to give to others, can be some of the most helpful "tools" we can share with those around us.

We don't know what others are going through until we share what we've been through or are working through now. You might be surprised to learn how many people are wearing masks that seem like they're "okay", when they're actually hurting, open to hearing kind, encouraging, loving truths from people who have healed from tough times.

That's right. Just like the favorite tools of mechanics, are the "tools" in givers' toolboxes of life shiny, pretty, and freshly purchased? Not hardly! Life "tools" are only gathered from experiences---positive and challenging. They're well-worn, nicked, and stained. And highly useful.

What life tools are in your toolbox? What lessons have you learned that you could share with others to help them avoid the same tough situations or to help them overcome those same challenges?

Like my friend, Kary Oberbrunner says, "Let your Pain become your Platform to help others heal." Share the Life Tools you've accumulated over the years, regardless of your age, in a way that helps people heal, grow, learn, or overcome---that helps them Win More at Life.

7) Gain

While #6 would be an excellent place to wrap this chapter up in a neat little bow, I would be remiss if I did not share the greatest reason why Chaz and I do everything we do with the goal of excellence.

Our personal faith.

It's our Deepest Why. I'm sure it is for many of you reading this book. No, I'm not going preach to you, I promise. I'll keep it simple.

For Chaz, me, and others with similar beliefs, intentionally pursuing a Win/Win life is the way we show our love for the One who made us, Who gave us a purpose beyond ourselves, Who blesses us with so many good things. We often remind ourselves that the quality of our lives, relationships, work, and fun are due to His kindness to us and those we love, and we want to pass that love along to others.

In everything we do, we want our words, actions, beliefs, and values to point to Him, our Heavenly Father, Who greatly loves us. Because of His love for us, we desire to express that love towards all those around us. It's most fulfilling to pour into the lives of those who feel like they can't, or truly cannot, give back. That's what a life of Love and Abundance looks like.

Because this is our Deepest Why, Winning More at Life has a very different feeling and meaning to it than our lives did when we were focused on ourselves as our greatest priority. Been there, done that. Never felt fulfilled, happy, or full of purpose.

If you were to talk with Chaz, me, or some of the other people I've interviewed, this deeply held value is a game changer for us.

We measure Winning at Life in a very different way---by what others receive from us AND from what we achieve. Both—The Genius of And, as Jim Collins calls it.

We do celebrate and appreciate achieving personal goals, while looking to see how those accomplished goals add to others' happiness, fulfillment, dreams, and growth.

This is an exceptional way to live your life, to Win More at Life. Let me leave you with one final thought....

Winning Secrets: Win/Win

My Menu

_____

_____

_____

_____

_____

_____

Conclusion

"The two most important days in your life are the day you were born and the day you find out why."

Mark Twain

Thank you for spending time with me. I sincerely hope that my encouraging words, all true!, resonated with you and inspired you to act, to never give up on pursuing your dreams. You **are** Winning at Life. We walked through several ways to Win **more** at Life. Keep doing that, for the rest of your life.

Worth sharing twice

In case you didn't notice, I repeated myself in this book. Did you happen to catch it? No, I'm not referring to the main theme of the book—what Winning More at Life looks like.

There were two stories that revealed more than one way to Win at Life: Joe Martin ditching a toxic customer who refused to treat his team member with respect---beliefs over business & John DiJulius' ingenious method to show someone you care about them—the F.O.R.D. approach.

Along with these 2 stories, we also learned that *how* we live our lives can absolutely be Heroic, when we do it with a Higher Purpose in mind and with Excellence.

The common element to both repeated stories and Heroic Success is how I concluded the book---about others. We truly, deeply Win at Life when we help others Win at Life, too.

Win/Win, best lived out, is when the first Win comes from encouraging and equipping others; the second Win is what we automatically receive from helping them Win at Life.

The most fulfilling life is the one that's focused on impacting lives around us. And then, one day, we look back and realize how wealthy we truly are. Not only because of what's in our bank accounts, but because of the rich, rewarding relationships with incredible people we're blessed to know.

More dollars don't automatically equal more Winning. More impact, more positive influence always equals Winning More at Life.

The spiritual principle that it is more blessed to give than to receive---it's true! Don't give to get; give to bless others. You'll receive far more than you could possibly imagine.

Lifelong Learning

Harry S. Truman once said, "Not all readers are leaders, but all Leaders are Readers." The love of learning is one of the most powerful ways to Win at Life. It keeps us curious, young, creative, others-focused, and never content with the status quo. You will never hear a lifelong learner say, "But that's the way we've always done it!"

If you're diligently pursuing reading for personal and professional growth, I'd be happy to share some of the incredible books I've read over the past few years. Just email me to request my Good Reads list at **john@7waysmenu.com**, and I'll send you the link to my Read bookshelf.

One of the most impactful reads of 2022 was Atomic Habits by James Clear. Without giving the key principles of James' book away, here's one of his life-changing tips in line with what we've explored about Winning at Life.

Choose one thing to improve every day and make it a habit. Just 1% improvement every day, with built-in positive habits, results in over 300% improvement by the end of one year. That's huge!

So, start with what the best definition of Winning at Life is, measure your progress with your own ruler, celebrate progress & milestones on your way to your

BHAG's. Then study and implement the other 7 tools we discovered. Whether it takes 10 months or 10 years to habitually implement these Winning principles into your life, doesn't matter. What matters most is: start Today and keep going! I'm proud of you for embracing Truth and abandoning toxic lies.

I need your help

Your feedback is much appreciated. I love to hear from readers about how my books have encouraged & equipped them. Check out my website, johndhanson.com, to learn about the ways I encourage people and businesses—through public speaking, workshops, and business coaching.

If you know a business owner, association, event manager, or business leader looking for workshops that shatter stale paradigms and infuse their people with purpose and encouraging insight, please share my website with them.

If you know a good friend or colleague who's struggling with life challenges, please share a copy of my book with them. Every time I read this, I'm encouraged to continue to chase my BHAG's, to never settle for "good enough." It would be a tremendous blessing to lift others up, to give them hope.

My next book!

Heroism---it's pulled at us since we were kids. Every culture has Heroes. It's part of our humanity—to aspire to greatness.

But is Heroism only reserved for Hollywood movies, the military, first responders, healthcare providers, and educators? Absolutely not!

And what about Leadership? There's TONS of books, courses, speakers, and training on Leadership. But what is it really?

Stay tuned! I'm already working on my next book, based on my most popular presentation---Heroic Leadership: Engage & Empower to Excel.

I truly believe that every person has the potential to be a highly effective Leader and be Heroic, no matter their role, career, responsibilities, talents, abilities, or giftedness.

Everyone can be a Heroic Leader. I'm eager to show you how.

Last Word

Get out there and Win more at Life! I'm cheering for you; we're all in this together.

Bibliography

Introduction

https://web.archive.org/web/20160822033050/https://www.
rio2016.com/en/athletics-standings-at-mens-100m

Chapter 1—What It Is & Whose Ruler

https://www.cnbc.com/2018/05/15/how-much-americans-
have-saved-for-retirement.html

http://www.baylorbears.com/sports/c-
track/mtt/trayvon_bromell_881966.html

http://www.usatf.org/Events---Calendar/2016/U-S--
Olympic-Team-Trials---Track---Field/Results.aspx

https://www.cnbc.com/2017/09/11/10-billionaires-who-
grew-up-dirt-poor.html

https://bleacherreport.com/articles/1040524-the-top-15-nfl-
hall-of-famers-who-never-played-in-a-super-bowl/#slide1

Whitelaw, Ian. "*A measure of all things: the story of man and measurement*", New York, NY, St. Martin's Press, 2007.

International Bureau of Weights and Measures (2006), *The International System of Units (SI)* (PDF) (8th ed.), *ISBN 92-822-2213-6, archived* (PDF) from the original on 2017-08-14

Chapter 2—Who Are You?

https://www.pbs.org/wgbh/nova/transcripts/2816miracle.html

https://health.clevelandclinic.org/why-giving-is-good-for-your-health/

https://www.nptrust.org/philanthropic-resources/philanthropist/giving-is-good-for-your-health/

https://www.cafonline.org/docs/default-source/about-us-publications/caf_wgi2018_report_webnopw_2379a_261018.pdf

https://givingusa.org/giving-usa-2017-total-charitable-donations-rise-to-new-high-of-390-05-billion/

https://www.cafonline.org/about-us/publications/2021-publications/caf-world-giving-index-2021

Chapter 3—When, Not If

https://qz.com/1136366/the-number-of-young-american-girls-turning-to-self-harm-is-skyrocketing/

https://www.apa.org/monitor/2015/07-08/who-self-injures

https://www1.cbn.com/700club/kary-oberbrunner-feeling-pain

https://ignitingsoulsconference.com/

https://www.dominican.edu; May 2015, "Study highlights strategies for achieving goals"

https://www.entrepreneursofcolumbus.com/cameron-mitchell-cameron-mitchell-restaurants/

https://www.briantracy.com/blog/personal-Success/Success-through-goal-setting-part-1-of-3/

https://publishingperspectives.com/2011/05/200-million-americans-want-to-publish-books/

https://www.twincities.com/2014/10/17/vikings-50-years-later-jim-marshalls-wrong-way-run-remains-an-nfl-classic/

Chapter 4—Will to Win

https://www.inc.com/carmine-gallo/how-james-dysons-
thousands-of-failures-can-help-you-tell-a-captivating-
founder-origin-story.html

https://failurebeforesuccess.com/kieran-behan/

Made in the USA
Monee, IL
17 November 2023

46719301R00131